Create the KITCHEN of a Lifetime

A step-by-step approach to develop your dream kitchen including Universal Design

Sylvie Meehan
Interior Designer, CAPS Certified Aging-in-Place Specialist

"Homes can be wonderfully adaptable places, accommodating a family's evolving needs as children grow up and homeowners grow older. You want your home to adjust to you, rather than you adjusting to your home."

—Sylvie Meehan

Hello!

I wanted to write this book because I want to simplify the design process of your kitchen, and to make you aware of the options you have. I want your home to adjust to you as you grow older, rather than you adjust to your home. This book includes step-by-step instructions to guide you through designing the perfect kitchen. You will also find some information on Universal Design so you can stay in your own home, no matter your age! Even if the concept of staying longer in your home is not for you, you will find so much more in the Discovery and Material section of this book to design your dream kitchen.

I hope this book will make the kitchen design process easy and enjoyable for you. I want you to also realize that you have a lot of possibilities with your own home so you can stay there longer and feel independent, safe, and comfortable.

CREATE THE KITCHEN OF A LIFETIME

A step-by-step approach to develop your dream kitchen including Universal Design

Sylvie Meehan Designs All rights reserved.
Published by Sylvie Meehan Designs, Fort Worth, TX
Copyright © 2011 by Sylvie Meehan

No part of this book may be reproduced by any mechanical, photographic, or electronic process or in the form of a phonographic recording; nor may it be stored in a retrieval system, transmitted, or otherwise be copied for public or private use—other than for "fair use" as brief quotations embodied in articles and reviews—without prior written permission of the publisher. For information, contact Sylvie Meehan Designs.

Telephone: (817) 913-5008
Email: smeehan@sylviemeehandesigns.com

www.sylviemeehandesigns.com

Limit of Liability/Disclaimer of Warranty: While the publisher and author have used their best efforts in preparing this book, they make no representations or warranties with respect to the accuracy or completeness of the contents of this book and specifically disclaim any implied warranties of merchantability or fitness for a particular purpose. No warranty may be created or extended by sales representatives or written sales materials. The advice and strategies contained herein may not be suitable for your situation. You should consult with a professional where appropriate. Neither the publisher nor author shall be liable for any loss of profit or any other commercial damages, including but not limited to special, incidental, consequential, or other damages.

Cover and Interior design: Toolbox Creative, www.ToolboxCreative.com

Library of Congress Cataloguing-in-Publications Data
Library of Congress Control Number: 2010907045
Sylvie Meehan
Create the kitchen of a lifetime
ISBN: 978-0-9845768-0-7
Printed in the United States of America.

2011

Table of Contents

DEDICATION	10
HOW TO USE THIS BOOK	11
CHAPTER 1: WORKING WITH A DESIGNER	12
Step 1: What Kind of Designer Do You Want, and Where Do You Find Your Designer?	16
Step 2: Homework	17
Style	17
Kitchen Lifestyle	18
Budget	18
Step 3: Telephone Calls	19
Step 4: Interviews with Designers	20
Step 5: The Designer Comes Back with a Design Proposal and Rough Ideas	24
Step 6: Choose the Designer You Want to Work with	24
Step 7: Turn in your homework	24
Step 8: The Designer Starts Creating Preliminary Drawings	25
Floor plan example	26
Perspective example	27
Step 9: Design Finalization	28
Step 10: Go Shopping	29
Step 11: The Final Meeting	30
CHAPTER 2: YOUR PERSONAL KITCHEN DISCOVERY	34
Step 1: House Flow	38
Public Rooms	38
Private Rooms	38
Step 2: The 6 Kitchen Zones	39
Non-consumable zone	40

Consumable zone 40

Preparation zone 40

Cooking zone. 40

Cleaning zone 40

Eating zone 40

Step 3: Kitchen Layouts 41

Step 4: What Do you Like About Your Kitchen? 46

Step 5: What Don't You Like About Kitchen? 47

Step 6: What is Your Kitchen Lifestyle? 48

Kitchen lifestyle questionnaire 50

Step 7: How Do You Find Your Style? 61

Step 8: Think About Your Budget 68

Example of budget for the kitchen remodel 69

CHAPTER 3: GROWING OLDER IN YOUR OWN HOME 76

Changing Demographics 79

The Baby Boomer Generation 80

What Happens As We Age? 80

Words of Wisdom. 81

CHAPTER: 4 WHAT IS UNIVERSAL DESIGN AND WHY IS IT IMPORTANT? . . . 84

What is Universal Design? 87

What are the Differences Between an Accessible House and a Universal Design House? 88

Introduction and Principles of Universal Design. 88

The Seven Principles of Universal Design 88

Plan Ahead. 89

Universal Design Features for the Kitchen 90

Cabinets 90

Countertops 91

Backsplashes 91

Flooring 92

Appliance Fixtures 92

Plumbing Fixtures 94

Lighting Fixtures 95

Hardware Fixtures 95

Walls 96

Glass 96

Fabric 96

Storage 96

Windows 96

Safety 96

Hallways 97

Heating, Ventilation, and Air Conditioning 97

Reduced Maintenance and Convenience Features 97

CHAPTER 5: STEPS OF DISCOVERY OF MATERIAL 100

Step 1: Color 104

Countertops 104

    NATURAL COUNTERTOP 105

    SYNTHETIC COUNTERTOPS. 108

    ECONOMIC OPTIONS 109

    COUNTERTOP ACCESSORY 110

    BASIC COUNTERTOP EDGES PROFILES. 110

Cabinets 114

    REFINISHING (PAINTING OR RESTAINING) CABINETS 115

    REPLACING WITH NEW CABINETS 115

    CONSTRUCTION 117

    MATERIAL 117

    STYLE 119

    COLOR 120

    ACCESSORIES 121

Backsplash 126

    SIZES 128

    PATTERNS. 128

    MATERIAL 128

    GROUT 132

    SEALER FOR GROUT 132

    SEALER FOR STONE 132

Flooring 134
    CERAMIC TILE 134
    GROUT 135
    SEALER FOR GROUT 135
    HARDWOOD 135
    LAMINATE 136
    NATURAL STONE 136
    SEALER FOR STONE 137
    VINYL 137

Walls, Ceilings, Doors and Trims 140
    PAINT 140
    STAIN 142
    WALLPAPERS 142

Step 2: Metal 149

Appliance Fixtures 149
    COLORS 150
    WOOD PANELED 151
    OTHER COLORS 151
    REFRIGERATORS 152
    ICE MAKERS 156
    FREEZERS 157
    WINE REFRIGERATORS 158
    RANGES 159
    WALL OVENS 162
    COOKTOPS 164
    WARMING DRAWERS 166
    MICROWAVE OVENS 167
    SPEED CONVECTION COOKING OVENS ... 169
    VENTING SYSTEMS AND HOODS 170
    DISHWASHERS 173
    COFFEE MACHINE 175
    TRASH COMPACTORS 176

Plumbing Fixtures 177
    FAUCETS 178
        Color 178
        Sprayer or Not 178
        Spout Height 179

		Handles	180
		Speciality Faucets	182
		Soap Dispenser	182
	BASIN SINKS		185
		Basin Sink Sizes	186
		Basin Sink Styles	187
		Basin Sink Finishes	189
	GARBAGE DISPOSALS		190
Lighting Fixtures			193
	GENERAL LIGHTING		194
	AMBIENT LIGHTING		195
	TASK LIGHTING		195
	ACCENT LIGHTING		196
Hardware Fixtures			198
	HARDWARE FOR CABINETS		198
	HARDWARE FOR INTERIOR DOORS		201

Step 3 Architectural 203

Window 203

Door 204

Molding 204

Ceiling and doorway Treatment 204

    CEILING TREATMENT 204

    DOORWAY TREATMENT 205

Step 4 Miscellaneous 206

Glass 206

Fabric 208

Luxury items 209

    HOME AUTOMATION 209

    INTERNET AND EMAIL 209

    SMART PHONE 209

    CAD (COMPUTER-AIDED DESIGN) 210

    BONUS: OUTSIDE KITCHEN 210

CONGRATULATIONS! 215

REFERENCES 216

ABOUT THE AUTHOR 217

Dedication

This book is dedicated to all of the men and women who would like to enjoy their kitchen. I want to help families come together again in the kitchen and help families stay in their own homes as they grow older. My belief is, if you feel happy in your kitchen, you will want to spend more time in there and invite people over.

The kitchen has always been the "gathering place," the one room in the house where everyone came together. This was where grandchildren learned to bake cookies, where secrets were told while washing dishes. This was where recipes were exchanged and culinary skills were bragged about. The kitchen has always been the heart of the home.

Today, though, so many people are ordering fast food, going out to the restaurant, or buying frozen meals from the grocery store. What about making memories? What about family time? What about eating healthy food? My heart's desire is to enable all of you to enjoy time in your kitchen as you prepare lovely meals or entertain your friends and family more frequently.

Watching TV while eating will not create memories. At least one or two times a week, try not doing that. You will be glad you did, and create beautiful memories with your loved ones.

This book—my first—is also dedicated to my mother. She taught me how to care for others, be helpful and be respectful to others. She always tells me I will accomplish everything I want if I set my mind to it. She is supporting me on everything I want to do. She is an inspiration and I love her dearly. Merci beaucoup Maman.

How to use this book

This book has been divided into 5 chapters. In chapter 1 explains the steps when working with a designer. Chapter 2 will guide you step by step to discover what you like and don't like, how to find your kitchen lifestyle, style and budget, and to put together your wish list.

Chapters 3 and 4 include information on Growing older in your home and what is Universal Design. Keep this section in mind and think about these concepts when you get to the material section later in the book.

Chapter 5 is where you actually design your dream kitchen. Chapters 2 and 5 of the book will be developed by you. I carefully guide you through each step of the process, so you know exactly where to start and what to do next. I hope you will write all over those pages. Highlight the parts you want to be sure to remember, make notes in the margins, underline sentences, and circle words. I have included lots of blank pages for you to write on. When you get ideas, write them down. When you see pictures of rooms and design elements you like, cut them out and paste them in here. When you find paint color swatches or fabrics you like, glue them in. Make this book a journal and a scrapbook of your dreams, wishes, thoughts, and plans. Take all the time you need, don't rush, and enjoy the process.

This book has been designed so you can feel like I am right there with you, discussing your kitchen lifestyle over a cup of coffee or a glass of wine in your kitchen. Together we will work through each step of your design; we'll decide what you would like to have changed, and talk about everything from colors to textures to fixtures.

In this section I want to help you understand the steps when working with a designer. The more comfortable you are with the process, the more successful the project will be.

Steps of Working With a Designer

STEP 1
What Kind of a Designer?

STEP 2
Homework

STEP 3
Telephone Calls

STEP 4
Interviews with Designers

STEP 5
The Designer Will Come Back with Proposal and Rough Ideas

STEP 6
Chose Your Designer

STEP 7
Turn in Your Homework

STEP 8
Preliminary Drawings

STEP 9
Design Finalization

STEP 10
Go Shopping

STEP 11
Final Meeting

CHAPTER ONE

Understand how the designer works so you can be comfortable with the process.

First, I would like to say that every designer has

his/her own approach when doing design. The process I have used in this book is the method that works best for me — other designers will have their own methods. Designers are all similarly trained, but when they start working and gaining experience, their style becomes more defined. A designer who is trained by an interior design firm will have a much different approach than a designer who works with a remodeling company.

The important thing is for you to understand how the designer usually works — you need to be comfortable with the process. The designer will help you clarify your style and kitchen lifestyle, then help you design a beautiful, functional home right down to selecting all of your materials. A designer will help you remodel your current home or plan a future home. You may ask your designer to manage the project alone, or you may wish to hire a remodeler or a handyman if the project is very small. The person in charge of the project will obtain all required permits and must have liability insurance.

You don't need to redo your kitchen completely to benefit from a designer. You may want to change the floor, countertop and backsplash only — we call this a partial remodeling. It is not as easy as it may seem; you will need to make sure your new material will match the existing ones. Believe me, this could be very challenging if the existing materials don't already match together.

Let's go step-by-step so you can see what is involved in working with a designer:

STEP 1
What Kind of Designer Do You Want, and Where Do You Find Your Designer?

First of all, we need to clarify something—designers are often confused with "decorators," but there is a difference.

Interior designers are trained for designing the inside of a home in accordance with construction and building code requirements; their education involves thorough training for structural elements, such as construction and functional as well as aesthetic appearance.

Decorators work primarily on the aesthetic appearance of a room, and their education is more along the lines of art and visual effects.

Kitchen designers are similar to interior designers, but they specialize in kitchen design.

So, where do you find your designer? Now that you understand the difference between designing and decorating, how do you look for the designer you would like to work with? Start by asking for personal recommendations from your family and friends—ask them how their experience with that designer was. Otherwise, you can also research the Internet for designers in your area. There are websites where you can prescreen designers at no cost to you. Try to limit yourself to choosing between no more than three designers, or the decision could be overwhelming.

Trust your instincts and go with the one you feel comfortable sharing your ideas with and who you feel will listen to you. And, of course, keep what their references said in mind.

STEP 2
Homework

Before scheduling a meeting with potential designers, you need to have done some preparation ahead of time—this is what I call your homework. By doing your homework now, you will save time with your designer in the first meeting.

STYLE

What are you attracted to? Look at magazines and on the Internet; look at homes around your city, and look at the kitchens of your friends and family. Cut out or print pictures of things you like and place them in the Style section of the Discovery chapter.

KITCHEN LIFESTYLE

The next step is to think about your everyday schedule. What tasks do you do by yourself? What tasks do you share with your spouse or with your children? Do you have certain days to do specific tasks? Do you eat out for dinner or cook at home; do you cook alone or together? Write down all of your thoughts on the blank sheets in the kitchen Lifestyle section of the Discovery chapter.

> It is best to have all the decision makers of the home involved from the beginning of the process. I have worked with a client whose husband said to her, "What ever you want honey." As the project was moving along he stepped in and made changes. We had to start all over, redesign and choose other materials. To avoid that, have all the decision makers working with you from the beginning.

BUDGET

Planning a budget beforehand serves as a guide for your designer. The price of your home and the status of your neighborhood will have an effect on your budget. What are your expectations? It is very important to clarify them, because it is easy to get over budget. If you decide to splurge in one area, you may need to cut back on another. Your designer can tell you if your ideas can be accomplished and how big your budget will need to be.

Don't be afraid to share your budget with the designer; it doesn't mean they will spend your money left and right—it will guide them not to over or under design. If they don't respect your budget, say goodbye and interview another designer. If you have no idea how much your kitchen project may cost, think about what you can spend and ask the designer to give you a range. If you are up for a challenge, try to put together a preliminary budget, and go to the Discovery: Budget section later in this book. I have already listed some of the things you will need to think about.

> Don't worry if you can't figure out the budget part—the designer will help you with this.

STEP 3
Telephone Calls

Do your homework before calling a designer so you will be more prepared to answer their questions. Call the designer(s) you want to meet; telephone calls help to screen out the ones you don't feel comfortable with. When you call, tell the designer why you want to remodel or get a new home, and give them a rough description of the project to be done. Agree on a date and time to meet, and be sure to give them your address and contact information. Don't forget to check your spouse's schedule to make sure he or she can meet the designer also. The telephone call should last around 30 minutes.

Don't forget to ask the designer if the first appointment is free of charge. If it is free, the designer will ask more questions to understand what you want to accomplish, and could give you some ideas, but don't expect the designer to share all their ideas for free. If the designer charges a fee, the designer will give you ideas for your project at that time.

STEP 4
Interviews with Designers

Now it's time to meet the designers in person; the interview should last about one hour. Invite them to come to see your home, or the floor plan for the new home, and discuss some of your ideas with them. Ask to see their portfolio, their references, and call them later. This is an interview process for you—if you don't feel comfortable with that person, don't go any further—follow your instinct.

This is your opportunity to see if you and the designer are a good match. You should feel like you are with a friend who understands your needs and wishes. Your designer should be able to provide you with some rough ideas that are functional and practical. Discuss what is not working for you in your home, and tell your designer why you want to remodel or get a new home. You need to be very honest about everything, especially your likes, dislikes, and budget. If you don't get everything out in the open with your designer, the success of the project could be jeopardized.

Here are some things to discuss with the designer:

> Why do you want to update the room? Is it not as functional as you would like or does it look outdated?
>
> What are your style preferences?
>
> What is your kitchen lifestyle?
>
> Who lives in the house? How many children are there, and how old are they? Do your parents live with you? Do you have any pets?
>
> What is your budget?
>
> Do you have a deadline for the work to be done?

The designer needs to collect as much information as possible about what you want for your kitchen project so they can come back with a proposal that will be more accurate. Show them the "Discovery" section of this book. The designer may also want to take pictures of your kitchen and maybe measurements of the space.

After talking with the designer, you will probably have more ideas or more questions. Take time to write them down here:

_____
_____
_____
_____
_____
_____
_____
_____
_____
_____
_____
_____
_____
_____

STEPS OF WORKING WITH A DESIGNER

Be sure to talk to your designer before plans for your kitchen are finalized. If the foundation has already been poured, it will be too late or too costly to make changes. For example, if the drain for your kitchen sink has already been set in place, you won't be able to move the sink. If you do, it will cost a lot of money and will waste time.

NOTES AND QUESTIONS FOR THE DESIGNER:

_____
_____
_____
_____
_____
_____
_____
_____
_____
_____
_____
_____
_____
_____
_____
_____

NOTES AND QUESTIONS:

STEP 5
The Designer Comes Back with a Design Proposal and Rough Ideas

This is where the designer will come back with rough ideas and present possible plans for your project. If you are considering more than one, you will need to decide which designer you want to work with after this step — choose the person that you feel most comfortable with. Hopefully it's also the one who shows you the plan you like best. You want to feel like your designer fully understands what it is you want to do with your home. This is the step where the designer could give you an idea of how much the project will cost. As you make your decision, find out what the payment arrangements would be, and be sure to ask for references.

STEP 6
Choose the Designer You Want to Work with

After interviewing your designers, you will have to choose one. You will be asked to sign a contract and pay a retainer or deposit. If you are ready to move forward, you should sign the contract so they can get to work on the next step — creating your drawings!

STEP 7
Turn in your homework

You have chosen the designer you want to work with. This is the time you present all of the information you have collected in this book and the problem(s) you are having with your kitchen, and how you can apply Universal Design if you wish to do so. (Universal Design is discussed in chapter 4). Show everything to your designer and explain all of your thoughts and dreams. If you are building a new home and have a copy of the blue prints, or of the kitchen that needs work, you should give it to the designer at this point. If this option is not available, the designer will measure the kitchen in order to create a design that will be accurate.

STEP 8

The Designer Starts Creating Preliminary Drawings

The designer will take all of your ideas and notes back to their office and draw up the preliminary design. If you have an open concept floor plan, your designer will try to match what already exists. They will draw up floor plans for your cabinets, appliances, plumbing, and electrical fixtures, using all of your specifications, ideas, and wishes. The designer will create ideas that help you clarify your current and future needs. The designer should think of details you may have overlooked—that's why you hired them, right?

After putting together the preliminary design, your designer will provide ideas on what they can do with the workspace using your preferences for your style and kitchen lifestyle. Again, make sure the designer understands what you want—now is the time to adjust the design. Don't be afraid to ask for specific details; make sure you are on the same page.

At this point is where the excitement begins! Trust your designer to guide you through the process. If you don't feel excited, it is probably because the designer does not understand what you want to accomplish—share your concerns! Take time to think about what you want, and never agree to something if you don't feel good about it. Don't let the designer "force" you into anything.

When the preliminary design is done, your designer will check prices with their contractors or meet with your remodeler to figure out how much your project will cost. Sometimes the designer or the remodeler will present your allowances (or estimated cost) on the materials to be bought. This step helps you know if you are staying within the budget and, if necessary, make adjustments to the project.

The next two pictures show what a floor plan and perspective of your new kitchen could look like. Some designers or remodelers also do a floor plan of your existing kitchen.

FLOOR PLAN EXAMPLE

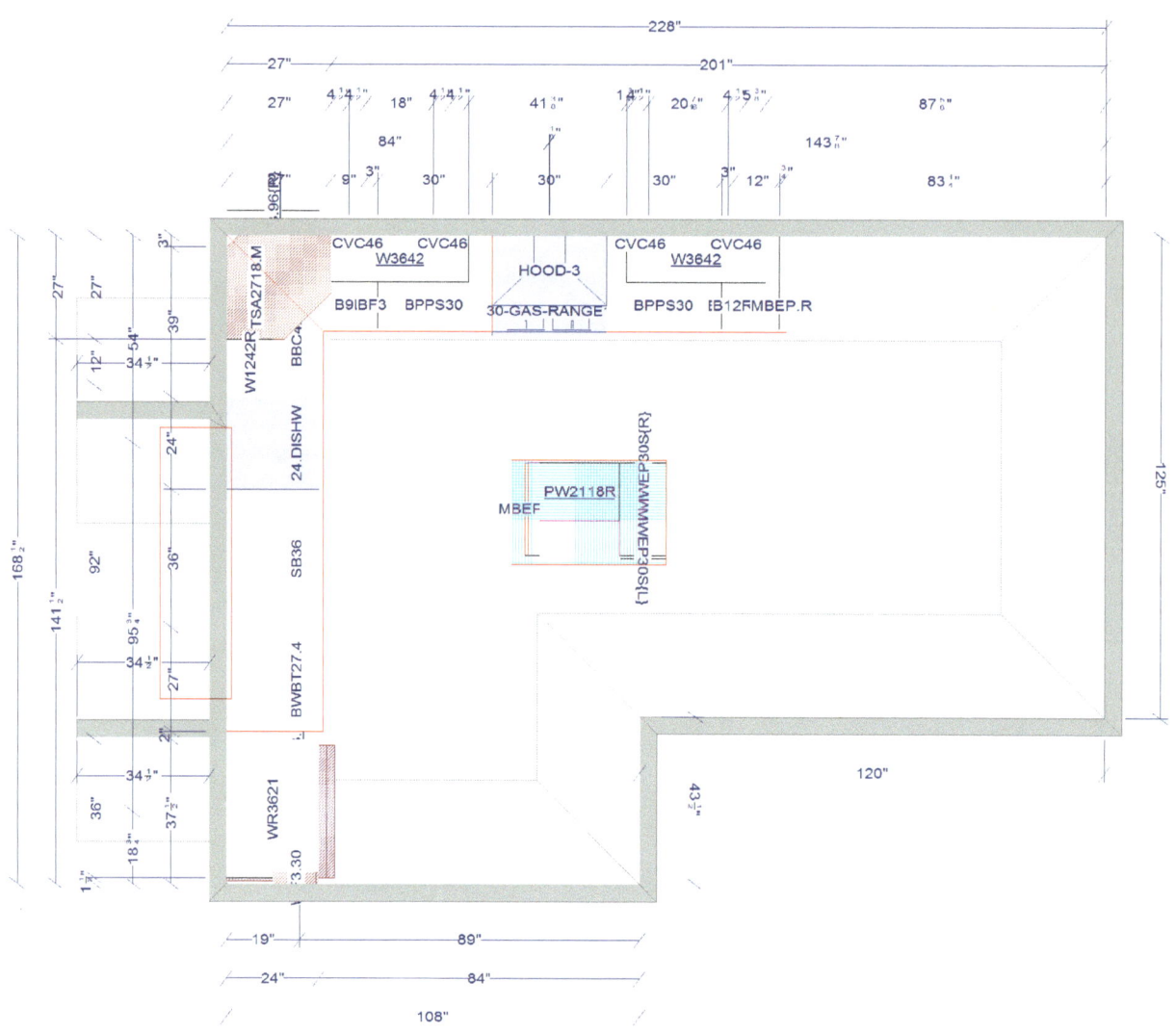

PERSPECTIVE EXAMPLE

Remember—to keep the cost of your remodeling down, keep the sink and refrigerator with water dispenser where they already are. Moving the plumbing can be expensive, especially if it's in a concrete slab. Moving the electrical and gas for your cooktop or range will also add to the cost. However, if money is not a concern, don't worry about any of these issues—this is your chance to correct the situation and get what you have always wanted.

STEP 9
Design Finalization

During this step, you and your designer will make revisions to your preliminary plan, make changes to your selections, and finalize the design. This is also the time where you will have a better idea of what your kitchen project will cost based on material allowances.

Take your time with this step and be sure that everything is exactly as you dreamed it would be. If you have any doubts about any of the plans, wait until you know exactly what it is you want. If necessary, refine the plan one more time.

STEP 10
Go Shopping

Now that your designer has a good idea of your style, kitchen lifestyle, and budget, and the design plan is done, it's time to go shopping. I take my clients to various showrooms to select all materials. The designer will know where to take you to, according to your style and budget. They have developed relationships with vendors and that will facilitate the process. You will see what is new at the store, and you'll learn a lot from your designer about what could work in your home and what can't, and why you should or should not choose it.

This is the fun part for almost every one of my clients! However, it can be overwhelming because there are so many choices to make, but your designer should help guide you through these choices. Just have fun and go to showrooms to explore. It is a fun learning experience, and for once, it's all about you and your kitchen! The designer will keep you on task with the project.

One thing needs to be pointed out—you will have to be careful not to overspend. It is so easy to be tempted and lose sight of the budget. Stay close to the allowances you have been given, or spend more on one item and less on another. Your designer should be very helpful.

Be sure to ask your designer to explain to you what kind of maintenance the materials you like will require.

I like to do the shopping by steps. In a perfect world you would start from scratch, like we do when building a new home. But in the remodeling world, that's not always the case, unless you are remodeling the whole house.

Let's say you are starting from scratch in your kitchen. You need to consider the colors in the adjacent room, such as your fireplace brick or stone, or the existing floor, or any material that is there to stay, especially if it is an open concept room. Definitely be careful of the floor in the room next to the kitchen since it will be touching the new floor.

Now let's say you are keeping your existing kitchen floor. Make sure your new material will match the existing floor, and choose the material in the order of the steps below. If you're not changing the material of one of the steps, just skip it.

First, choose the colors. If redoing the entire kitchen, start with the countertop then select the cabinet color (if it is a custom line), then the backsplash, the flooring, and finally, the paint color. All of these colors should coordinate with the countertop or your existing material from the other room.

> If you are buying stock cabinets with a limited choice of color, make this choice before choosing the countertop color.

We can accomplish more by starting where we have the fewest choices, then matching all of the rest to that. Be sure to bring along a piece of existing material like flooring or cabinet drawers to make sure it matches the new material. Get samples of the new material as well, so you can keep matching as you go.

STEP 11
The Final Meeting

At this meeting, your designer will give you drawings of your entire project, with spreadsheets showing all of the materials, vendors, and prices of your selections during your shopping time, and maybe pictures of what you selected so you can double check as they are installing the material. Check everything over closely to make sure it's exactly what you want, and then the designer or remodeler can tell you exactly how much your project will cost.

Did you know designers can also be hired as project managers? They can manage every aspect of the project, like buying materials, scheduling material purchases, contractors' time, and manage the execution of the project.

If you decide not to work with the designer for the execution of the project and decide to go with a remodeler, do the same steps you did when interviewing the designer in step 4 above, and choose the remodeler you want just as in step 6 above. You don't need to discuss every detail with the remodeler because, at this point, you will have the design and all material selected; just show them what the designer gave you and ask them to give you a bid, including the length of time it will take and what to expect during the construction phase.

Your designer should be available for questions during the remodeling process as the projects evolve. Trust me, you will have questions!

Your dreams are about to come true!

The steps in this section are so important—you need to understand your kitchen space, and what will work and what doesn't. You will need to be honest with this section. I called it Discovery because it is about you and your home. I will explain what a House Flow is and why this is important. We will learn about the kitchen zones and how they work and understand the layout of your kitchen. We will talk about what you like and don't like in your kitchen. In conclusion, what is your kitchen Lifestyle and Style, and follow with your budget. The later chapter on Material Selection is about what material is out there.

Your Personal Kitchen Discovery

STEP 1
Home Flow

STEP 2
The 6 Kitchen Zones

STEP 3
Kitchen Layouts

STEP 4
What Do You Like About Your Kitchen?

STEP 5
What Don't You Like About Your Kitchen?

STEP 6
What is Your Kitchen Life-style?

STEP 7
How Do You Find Your Style?

STEP 8
Think About Your Budget

CHAPTER TWO

"This is your scrapbook, your idea book, your dream catcher where you put all of your ideas and clippings and drawings and notes."

This is the fun part of the book! This is your scrapbook, workbook, ideas book—your "dream catcher" where you put all of your ideas, clippings, drawings and notes. This part of the book will go through each step of planning your kitchen and leave plenty of space for you to scribble your thoughts. I hope you have FUN with this!

What does the word "home" mean to you? For me, it is a reflection of who I am. My home is my sanctuary. How does your home feel to you? Ask yourself these questions:

> 1. Does my house reflect who I am?
>
> 2. Did I decide how it looks, or have I been influenced by others?
>
> 3. Is my home a place where I can retreat from the world and just be with my family and friends, or do I need a place to be re-energized?

Take a little time for yourself. Think about your relationship with your home.

What will make you enjoy your kitchen again and cook for your family and friends? What changes will need to be done?

To make your house a home, let's start by understand your space and finding what you like and don't like about your existing kitchen and your kitchen lifestyle.

The next step is to create a better design for the space. We call this "space planning." When you feel comfortable with the space planning or space layout (where the cabinets, appliances, plumbing and light fixtures go), then we'll work on the style and color of materials. The space planning is so important—if we make your room pretty and updated, but not functional, you will not enjoy it for a long time. Resist looking at the look only; think about the ease to use your kitchen and its functionality. You will have made every investment dollar worth it.

Do this section in the order that applies to you. Some people prefer to start with understanding what a budget looks like or their wish list before finding their kitchen lifestyle and style. The order is not important for this part.

> Your home should reflect who you are. Surround yourself and your family with what makes you happy.

STEP 1
House Flow

What is the "flow" of your home? Let's clarify where the public and private rooms are in the home so we can better understand the flow of the house.

Public Rooms	Private Rooms
Entry, kitchen, nook, family room, powder room, office, exercise room, media room, butler pantry, game room, formal dining, and formal living.	All bedrooms and all bathrooms relating to a bedroom. (I call it "personal room" as well).

House flow means all the colors need to flow for one room to another. It doesn't need to match perfectly, but you need to keep the flow in mind. If we start with an empty room, I ask my clients to show me a favorite picture, fabric, or object. This becomes our color inspiration; it shows me what they like and what color they are attracted to. If you are building a new home, make sure the color and style flow from one room to another for your public areas (see chart above). It is okay for your private rooms to be more unique, especially for kids—they need their bedrooms to adjust to them, too!

If you renovate your kitchen, always make sure you look at the color of the rooms adjacent to the kitchen. This is even more important if you have an open concept. Sometimes you have to continue or coordinate with the color you have in the other room, or start with the kitchen color if you plan to redo an adjacent room in the near future.

Also, consistent flooring makes the home look bigger. Watch for different thickness if you have different flooring—that can be hazardous to trip over.

When going shopping, bring along pieces of existing fabrics and colors to make sure it will match the new material. Put all of your samples in a bag and bring them along everywhere you go.

STEP 2
The 6 Kitchen Zones

My opinion on the work triangle is that is outdated. A work triangle means that the kitchen layout should be dictated by three points: the refrigerator, cooking area and sink, and all of them should be within easy reach. The kitchens now could be bigger and often have more than one cook. I like to design the kitchen around the way we will use it. Having all material handy when I prepare or cook a meal will save me time and frustrations. I like to design a kitchen using six zones instead. The six zones are:

NON-CONSUMABLE ZONE

This includes the dishes, glasses, silverware, pots and pans, plastic containers, books, and decorating items.

CONSUMABLE ZONE

Two parts:

Cold—food that must be refrigerated or frozen.

Room temperature—other foods such as pasta, rice, cereal, spices, and canned goods. Also called pantry, it can be built inside interior walls or built in the cabinetry.

PREPARATION ZONE

The area that requires lots of countertop space on which to spread out your ingredients, such as spices, mixing bowls, utensils, and small electrical appliances and also storage inside the cabinets for those accessories.

COOKING ZONE (ALSO KNOWN AS THE COOKING APPLIANCE ZONE)

This zone includes the microwave, cook top, and oven. Spices, oils, pots and pans used most frequently are also in this zone.

CLEANING ZONE

The sink, dishwasher, trash and recycle bins, plastic containers, plastic wrap, and cleaning supplies.

EATING ZONE

This zone means a countertop area, such as an island or peninsula or a table in the kitchen.

You will not be able to plan for the perfect zone every time. The layout of the kitchen is based on the architectural design (like wall, window and door placement) and will greatly affect the design zones. Do the best you can and it should be better than what you have right now.

STEP 3
Kitchen Layouts

Kitchen floor plans commonly include one of the following:

One Wall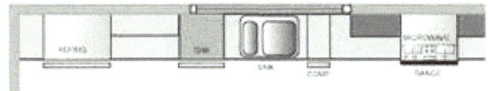

Corridor (also known as galley)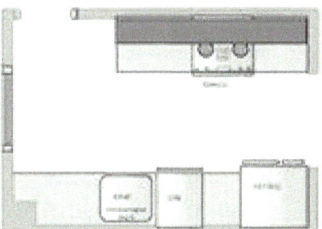

"L" shape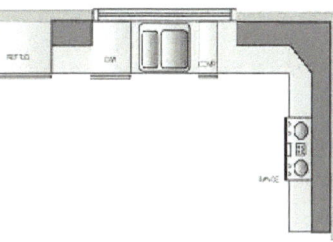

Double "L"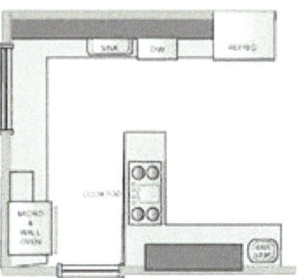

Drawings courtesy of Kitchens.com

"U" Shaped

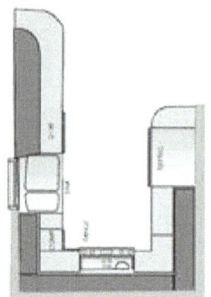

"G" Shaped

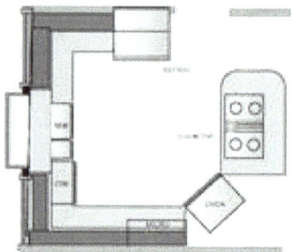

Drawings courtesy of Kitchens.com

Which floor plan do you have in your existing kitchen?

If you're remodeling your kitchen, the structure of your existing home will limit your layout options. You'll have more flexibility with larger spaces. Of course, if you're building a new home or adding on, you can design your kitchen however you want.

When looking at other kitchens for inspiration, keep in mind the layout of your kitchen. An "L" shape doesn't look like a "U" shape. You can modify your existing layout if it is not efficient for you, but keep in mind that more expense is involved if you move plumbing or electrical devices.

SKETCH A PICTURE OF YOUR EXISTING LAYOUT HERE OR CIRCLE ONE ON THE PREVIOUS TWO PAGES:

PICTURES OF YOUR EXISTING KITCHEN—INCLUDE SEVERAL VIEWS IF POSSIBLE:

PICTURES OF YOUR EXISTING KITCHEN—INCLUDE SEVERAL VIEWS IF POSSIBLE:

STEP 4
What Do you Like About Your Kitchen?

STEP 5
What Don't You Like About Kitchen?

STEP 6
What is Your Kitchen Lifestyle?

Your kitchen lifestyle is very important to making your house a home. It is defined by asking questions like these (feel free to write your answers and thoughts down):

Write down everything you can think of on the next few pages. Take as much time as you need. Ask your family to write their "wish lists" down too. Don't think about the budget at this time; that comes later. This section is all about discovery, not making decisions on what you can or can't afford.

Find a way to improve whatever stresses you or makes you unhappy in your home. You need to be happy about coming home from a long day at work. You need to be comfortable if you are home all day. Life is too short; don't wait until you realize you haven't lived the way you deserve.

DARE TO BE DIFFERENT. DARE TO BE YOU.

If you and your spouse feel strongly about how your home should look or feel, but you have different opinions, you might want to think about hiring a designer to save your marriage. Several of my clients have told me I saved their marriages. A good designer will listen to what both of you tell them about your tastes and needs, and will create a design to accommodate both of you by compromising so no one feels left out of the process. When your home reflects who you and your family members are, everything is perfect.

How do I live every day? What activities, other than cooking, do I like to do in the kitchen? (TV, computer, homework for kids, pay bills, etc.)

_____
_____
_____
_____
_____

Do I buy groceries every day, every week, once a month, or in bulk? Is my pantry big enough?

_____
_____
_____
_____
_____

Do I like to cook? Or eat out?

_____

Do I have kids? What ages?

_____

Does my parent live with us or visit often?

_____

Are my cook top, oven, fridge and freezer big enough?

_____

Am I right-handed or left-handed?

_____

How tall am I?

_____

Do I have any physical limitations? If yes, which ones?

_____
_____
_____

If I like to cook, does my kitchen function like it needs to do?

_____
_____
_____

If I like to entertain, does my kitchen accommodate several people at once to eat or help out? If not, what area is a problem?

_____
_____
_____

Does my spouse or children help with cooking?

_____
_____
_____

How tall are my helpers?

_____
_____
_____

Are my helpers right-handed or left-handed?

_____
_____
_____

YOUR PERSONAL KITCHEN DISCOVERY

Do my helpers have physical limitations? If yes, which ones?

_____
_____
_____

Do I have a collection? If yes, of what?

_____
_____
_____

How do I want to display my collection?

_____
_____
_____

Is my kitchen functional enough? If not, where does it need help?

_____
_____
_____

Where do I stand the most as I cook, by the stove or by the sink?

_____
_____
_____

Do I eat in the kitchen or in the dining room?

_____
_____
_____
_____
_____

Do I like to entertain?

_____
_____

Is my home designed for entertaining?

_____
_____
_____

How many guests do I usually invite?

_____
_____
_____

Am I a pack rat? If yes, of what?

_____
_____
_____

Do I have enough storage in my kitchen? If not, for what?

_____
_____
_____

What is difficult to store in my cabinets and drawers?

_____
_____
_____

YOUR PERSONAL KITCHEN DISCOVERY

Do I like to have my things out on the counter or put away in the cabinets?

_____
_____
_____

Is my kitchen easy to clean? If not, what is difficult?

_____
_____
_____
_____

Are my appliances easy to clean?

_____
_____
_____
_____

Are my appliances easy to clean? If not, which ones?

_____
_____
_____
_____

Am I the kind the person who is always looking for my cell phone?

_____
_____

Do I need places for more organization, like for paying bills and other tasks? If yes, for what tasks?

_____
_____
_____

Do I need to change the entire kitchen layout, or can I just reorganize to make better use of the space I have?

_____

_____

Is my kitchen large enough, or do I need to make an adjoining room smaller or add an addition?

_____

_____

Do I have enough electrical outlets?

_____

_____

Do I like to watch TV in the kitchen?

_____

_____

Is there enough light in the kitchen? If not, where do I need more?

_____

_____

_____

Where do I want to keep my cookbooks and recipes?

_____

_____

Do I like coffee or wine?

_____

_____

YOUR PERSONAL KITCHEN DISCOVERY

PUT PICTURES IN HERE IF YOU WANT TO — A PICTURE IS WORTH A THOUSAND WORDS.

Having all of this together in one place will make things a lot easier when the time comes for you to tell your designer what you like.

WRITE DOWN YOUR LIFESTYLE PREFERENCES OR PICTURES YOU LIKE:

WRITE DOWN YOUR LIFESTYLE PREFERENCES OR PICTURES YOU LIKE:

WRITE DOWN YOUR LIFESTYLE PREFERENCES OR PICTURES YOU LIKE:

___

YOUR PERSONAL KITCHEN DISCOVERY

WRITE DOWN YOUR LIFESTYLE PREFERENCES OR PICTURES YOU LIKE:

STEP 7
How Do You Find Your Style?

Examples of style are Old World, French, Traditional, Transitional, Zen, Contemporary, etc. You will feel more connected to your home when you find the style you like. It is easy to find examples by looking in magazines, on TV, and browsing the Internet. Just write the style you are attracting to or glue pictures.

You don't have to choose only one style. Instead, follow what is pleasant to you. If it is a mix of several styles (also called "eclectic"), you will need more skill to put it all together or it can look very messy. The pieces need to relate to each other; it might be the color scheme or the form, but something needs to make a connection. The exception is the unexpected piece, but that is an advanced subject for your designer to help you with.

What is the architectural style of your home? Do you want the new kitchen to reflect this style?

This is a question I have been asked a lot. Do I need to keep the same style for my kitchen as the rest of my house? The answer is not easy. A lot of designers will tell you to stay consistent with the rest of the house but, for me, it will depend on two things:

Do you plan to resell the house or keep it for as long as you want? If you want to resell it, keep the same style, but with an updated look. If you plan to stay there for a longer time, "please yourself." Don't go drastic—consider doing an eclectic style, (mixing different styles together). This is a more complicated task to achieve than you may think, so ask a designer for guidance; you don't want the look to clash. Don't forget the information on the flow of a home you just read. In the end, you want your home to reflect what you like—just be careful in mixing styles.

Be careful when watching home TV shows—they are not always realistic about their projects. Sometimes the cost is different because they only included the cost of materials and the labor was free. Sometimes the duration of the project is not accurately portrayed because not all the work involved was shown.

While the home TV shows are a great resource for ideas, you should check with your designer before you do anything. That wonderful idea might look perfect on TV, but it might not be right for your home. Your home might be bigger or smaller, lighter or darker, or have different architecture. Write ideas down that you like, but check with your designer before buying anything just in case it won't work well in your home.

If you did see something you liked, go to the home TV show website, find the show and episode you liked — they may have pictures posted of what you saw on that show that you can print and put in this book. Many times I've heard, "I saw that on TV and it looked so good…Save yourself that trouble by visiting their website.

Print pictures off the Internet and stick them between these pages. Cut out pictures from magazines and put them in here. Go "shopping" at other people's houses, and write down all of the things you like about those pictures and homes.

To help define what you like about style, just find what appeals to you; don't analyze what you see. Think about what your dream home looks and feels like. Let your imagination go—what do you see? What color are the walls? Is there a fireplace? Are there lots of windows? Do you want to use a design theme? What colors do you like? What things didn't you like? What do you like about your friends' kitchens? By selecting all that appeals to you, a style or pattern will emerge from page to page. Think of this as a journey; take all the time you need, and enjoy the process of discovery with a glass of wine or a cup of coffee in a comfortable chair.

When looking at pictures don't analyze them. Just pick the ones that are attractive to you. When you review the pictures you like, you will see a pattern emerge, like all the cabinets are white or dark countertop, etc. Be careful not to print every picture you like, it could cost you a lot on printer ink. Just choose your favorite ones.

PUT PICTURES OF STYLES YOU LIKE HERE AND ON THE NEXT FEW PAGES:

PICTURES OF STYLES YOU LIKE:

YOUR PERSONAL KITCHEN DISCOVERY

PICTURES OF STYLES YOU LIKE:

PICTURES OF STYLES YOU LIKE:

YOUR PERSONAL KITCHEN DISCOVERY

STEP 8
What is your budget?

Setting up your budget ahead of time is critical. You don't want to start a project without knowing exactly what the cost will be. You want to make this experience as stress-free as possible. Always add 10% extra for that unexpected problem or for something you really want to get, like special light fixtures or an unusual sink. Also, you never know what you may find behind the walls that can cost you more in labor.

How long do you plan to stay in your home? This will influence how much you should spend. Consider the value of your home versus the other homes in your neighborhood, especially if you plan on selling in the near future.

How much of your existing kitchen are you able to keep or re-use? Do you need new appliances, flooring, or cabinets? Can you refinish or repaint the cabinets you already have?

Before selecting all your material, you need to have an idea of how much your project could cost. You can accomplish that with allowances on material and labor. See an example of a budget on the next page. The designer or remodeler can help with that but they will need to know what you want to accomplish as precisely as possible.

> Remember—avoid extra expenses by keeping plumbing fixtures, such as the sink and refrigerator, in the same place as they are now, and look around to see if there is anything you can recycle or re-use from your existing kitchen.

Don't buy anything until you have prices on everything and you know much the project will cost. You can modify by spending less in one area and more elsewhere. If you are buying here and there you may lose control of the expenses.

An example of a kitchen budget for you to use or to get a better understanding of what cost is involved in your project, is on the next few pages.

EXAMPLE OF BUDGET FOR THE KITCHEN REMODEL

Item		Quantity	Estimated Cost or allowances	Actual Cost	Done
Permit	Permit if needed				
Demo	Dumpster for demo and to haul debris				
Frame work	Framing if adding or removing walls with sheetrock				
Walls	Paint or wallpaper material				
	Labor: Tape and bedding if needed				
	Labor: Texture if needed				
	Labor: Paint or stain				
	Labor: Wallpaper if needed				
Ceiling	Paint				
	Labor: same as walls above				
Cabinets	Materials				
	Trims				
	Accessories				
	Labor installation, paint or stain them				
Counters	Material				
	Labor install and undermount sink if needed				
Backsplash	Material				
	Labor				

YOUR PERSONAL KITCHEN DISCOVERY

EXAMPLE OF BUDGET FOR THE KITCHEN REMODEL

	Item	Quantity	Estimated Cost or allowances	Actual Cost	Done
Flooring	Material				
	Labor				
Appliances	Cook top or range				
	Oven				
	Refrigerator				
	Microwave				
	Hood				
	Dishwasher				
	Warm drawer				
	Coffee machine				
	Labor: installation				
Plumbing fixtures	Sink(s)				
	Faucets				
	Garbage disposal				
	Water filter cold/ hot				
	Labor: Rough (behind the wall) and Trim (what you see)				
Lighting fixtures	Recessed cans				
	Pendant light				
	Inside, below and above wall cabinets				
	Others like plugs and switches with dimmers				
	Labor: Rough (behind the wall) and Trim (what you see)				

EXAMPLE OF BUDGET FOR THE KITCHEN REMODEL

Item		Quantity	Estimated Cost or allowances	Actual Cost	Done
Hardware fixtures (main doors and cabinets	Material (pulls/knobs)				
	Labor				
Glass	Cabinets door				
	Labor				
Windows or doors	Material				
	Labor				
Luxury					
Unexpected Costs	Always add 10%				
Prepare for expenses like more restaurants					
Total Project					

What is your budget now after seeing all that is included in the remodel process?

$ _____

YOUR PERSONAL KITCHEN DISCOVERY

71

BUDGET NOTES:

BUDGET NOTES:

Where do you see yourself in 10, 20, or 30 years? As you move through life, will your kitchen be able to accommodate your changing lifestyle? In this section we will explain the aging of the population.

Growing Older In Your Own Home

CHANGING DEMOGRAPHICS

THE BABY BOOMER GENERATION

WHAT HAPPENS AS WE AGE?

WORDS OF WISDOM

CHAPTER THREE

"The perfect home will provide a haven in which you can grow older and still maintain your independence."

Our aging population is living longer than ever.

Some of the baby boomers are beginning to wonder where they are going to live. Some of the elderly are wondering where to stay in order to receive the care they need. I want to help all of these people learn how to make their homes more accessible so they can easily come and go from each other's houses. I want to help the baby boomer generation plan so they can have their parents come and live with them.

Some of my clients just love where they live. They know they can ask their neighbors to watch their dogs when they go on vacation. They like the location of their neighborhood in their cities. They are close to their favorite stores. They don't want to move as they get older. They just need their homes to be easier for them.

People don't like having to move if they don't need to.

CHANGING DEMOGRAPHICS

At the beginning of the 20th century, the average human lifespan was only 47 years. People with spinal cord injuries had only a 10% chance of survival. Most people with chronic conditions had to live in a care facility.

Today, people are better off financially and are living longer than at any time in history. Data shows that the average lifespan has increased to 76 years of age, largely due to healthier living, better medicine and vaccines, and proper sanitation. Nearly 80% of the population now lives past the age of 65. Projected estimates show that the number of people 65 years old and over will grow to almost 40 million by 2010. Compare that figure with the number at the end of World War II, when only one in 500 lived to 100 years of age!

In addition, more people are living with a disability of some sort. There are veterans of two world wars and multiple smaller wars still living. Antibiotics and other medical advances have enabled people to survive accidents and illnesses which would have been fatal before this era.

Demographics show a population that is older and more disabled than many realize, and this trend will continue. That's where Universal Design will help; Universal Design elements are a result of the growing awareness of the aging populace and their needs.

THE BABY BOOMER GENERATION

Statistics show that the baby boomer generation will jump from 45 million to more than 70 million by the year 2020. Baby boomers prefer to be cared for in their own homes rather than moving to assisted-living facilities. They see their own parents aging and having to depend on others in assisted care homes, and they don't want that lifestyle for themselves if there is any way they can avoid it.

Here are some reasons the baby boomers don't want to go to a nursing or assisted living home:

- Loss of independence
- Loss of the lifestyle to which they are accustomed
- Horror stories of the care provided by nursing home staff
- Very costly, leaving less money for their future and inheritance for their children

WHAT HAPPENS AS WE AGE?

As we age, all of us experience gradual declines in physical strength, flexibility, dexterity, and endurance. In general, we can expect the following to happen to some degree:

- Vision loss—changes in vision begin to happen after age 50, and by the time we reach 65, that may become more severe. Research shows that 1 in 20 people are legally blind by the time they are 85 or older. The lens of the eye becomes opaque and yellow, affecting our ability to see things as clearly as we used to, and it takes longer for eyes to focus.

- Hearing loss—this is the most common occurrence in people as they age. The conductivity of inner ear bones and nerve sensitivity begins to fade. Higher frequencies become harder to hear, and background noises become more interfering.

- Hand limitations—arthritis causes pain in the joints and limits dexterity.

Range of reach—we may need to use wheelchairs or walkers as we age—this limits how far we are able to reach while cooking or cleaning.

Disorientation/dizziness—many people experience dizzy spells as they get older, but for those who live with chronic dizziness, even the most familiar surroundings become intimidating.

Reduced mobility—walking and going up or down stairs becomes more difficult, especially if we have a heart or breathing disorder.

Loss of upper arm strength—affecting reach and agility.

WORDS OF WISDOM

Make sure your family knows your wishes for when you are older, including whether you want to move to a smaller home or stay where you are.

Think about your retirement funds. Houses must be maintained, and don't forget to add that cost to your financial plan for retirement. You may wish to start an account that will be used solely for taking care of your home.

Do some renovations on your home when you are younger, and think ahead to your needs as you grow older—you may wish to do your renovations in phases and stay within a smaller budget.

Consider doing bigger expense items while you are still employed, such as replacing roofs, septic tanks, water heaters, and cooling units.

Start or maintain a healthy lifestyle; exercise, eat healthy, and avoid stress as much as possible. Find what helps you relax and do it on a regular basis—the less medical expenses you have, the more you can afford these changes to your home. The healthier you are, the longer you will be able to stay in your own home.

There is a way to help you stay in your home longer—it is called "Universal Design," which is what will be discussed in the next chapter.

In this section I want to show you more about the option of being independent and still living in your home as you get older—this is referred to as "Universal Design." By incorporating Universal Design into your home now, your home will be able to adapt to your life changes as you grow older.

What is Universal Design and Why is it Important?

WHAT IS UNIVERSAL DESIGN?

WHAT ARE THE DIFFERENCES BETWEEN AN ACCESSIBLE HOUSE AND A UNIVERSAL DESIGN HOUSE?

INTRODUCTION AND PRINCIPLES OF UNIVERSAL DESIGN

PLANNING AHEAD

UNIVERSAL DESIGN FEATURES FOR THE KITCHEN

CHAPTER FOUR

"By incorporating Universal Design into your home now, your home will be able to adapt to your life changes as you grow older."

WHAT IS UNIVERSAL DESIGN?

Universal Design is a concept that provides safety and accessibility for people of all ages, from the very young to the elderly. It is helpful for people who are disabled as well as those with other physical challenges, such as those who are very tall or very short.

Examples of the elements of Universal Design are:

- Single-lever faucets, which are easier to use than knobs for those with arthritis.

- Thresholds that are flat or very low so they don't cause stumbles.

- Rooms that are very open with large doorways and passageways to provide easy access for wheel chairs or walkers.

- The kitchen areas include an extra five foot space for turning wheelchairs or walkers around with ease—if an island makes this difficult, consider removing it.

- Light switches that are installed lower on walls than the standard, so they can be easily reached by someone seated in a wheelchair.

- Electrical outlets that are installed higher than the standard, so they can be easily reached by people in wheelchairs.

- Faucets and drawer hardware that are easy to grip.

- Cabinet hardware that is easy to grip and pull, which knobs are not.

- Appliances that are located where they can be used while standing or seated.

- Appliance controls that are easy to understand and reach.

- Extra lighting in the kitchen, such as more windows and task lights.

- Windows that are easy to open/close.

- Work surfaces at varying heights to allow for use whether seated or standing.

- Flooring that is smooth and skid-resistant.

WHAT ARE THE DIFFERENCES BETWEEN AN ACCESSIBLE HOUSE AND A UNIVERSAL DESIGN HOUSE?

"Accessible" usually refers to people who are disabled and is a small part of the Universal Design concept; Universal Design covers the entire theory and exceeds the minimum standard required by code. A house built with Universal Design is for everyone, whereas an accessible house usually is built to address specific needs.

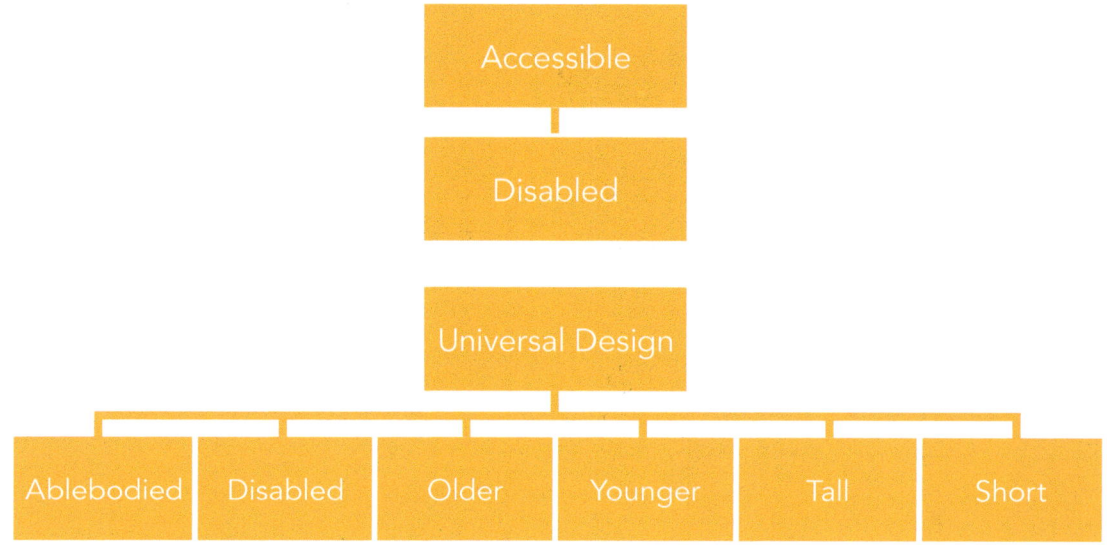

INTRODUCTION AND PRINCIPLES OF UNIVERSAL DESIGN

Universal Design meets the needs of all people. It also recognizes that abilities change over time.

THE SEVEN PRINCIPLES OF UNIVERSAL DESIGN

1. Unbiased use—the design is marketable to people with diverse abilities.

2. Flexible use—the design accommodates a wide range of individual preferences and abilities, such as both right-handed and left-handed use.

3. The design is simple—it's easy to understand, regardless of the user's experience, knowledge, language skills, or current concentration level.

4. Perceptible Information—the design can be used by people with impaired vision.

5. Tolerance for error—hazards are minimized through the use of such features as child locks on appliances.

6. Low physical effort—can be used efficiently and comfortably with a minimum of fatigue.

7. Sufficient size and space for use—appropriate room is provided regardless of the user's body size, posture, or mobility.

> Always try to use materials that require little or no maintenance.

PLAN AHEAD

Baby boomers are beginning to think about where they want to live during their golden years. If they want to stay independent in their own homes, Universal Design can help accomplish this. Keep Universal Design concepts in mind as you think about building or renovating your home at any age. Consider making some of these changes while you are still working and have access to more financial resources.

Did you know that relatives provide 80% of the care for their elderly family members? You may need to have your home ready in case you decide to do that.

> **You can start by remodeling your kitchen with Universal Design in mind and slowly renovate the other rooms in your home as the need arises. In the long run, you will save money by not waiting until the changes are needed to do this.**

When deciding on a designer to work with, make sure the designer is educated in Universal Design and has CAPS (Certified Aging in Place Specialist) certification. The CAPS certification verifies that these designers have been trained to help older generations stay safe, independent, and comfortable, regardless of their income or physical ability, as they age in the familiar surroundings of "home."

UNIVERSAL DESIGN FEATURES FOR THE KITCHEN

There are things you can do in your home to make it friendlier as you age. Think about the ideas I've listed on the next few pages, and how might they work for you

Decide and circle which Universal Design features you would like in your kitchen:

CABINETS

Make sure you have enough room to move a wheelchair or walker around. (you may need to remove the island).

Use more base cabinets and fewer wall cabinets.

Pull-out trays are better in base cabinets.

Pull-down shelves are helpful.

Add wall supports.

Upper cabinets should be lower than standard height.

Consider glass on cabinet fronts to see better what is inside.

Use open shelving for items that are used most often.

Roll-outs or drawers that are easy to access without having to bend over to see what's inside.

Avoid blind corner cabinets that you can't easily reach into or see what's in there.

Think about use of "zones" so everything is within reach, depending on the task.

Consider eliminating an island to provide more room to move around if the place is tight.

Seated work areas by counters need to be open underneath.

COUNTERTOPS

Enough space next to the oven, microwave, refrigerator, and cook top or range to put things on.

Non-scraping surfaces to slide hot pots from the stove to the counter.

Avoid sharp corners.

Accents on the edges make them easier to see.

Countertops should have various heights (e.g. 36" for a standard work surface and 32" for a child or seated person).

> It is less expensive to build a new home with the Universal Design concepts than modify your existing home. Think of modifications that will need to be done, such as enlarge doorways and doors, for example, and the time it will take to renovate while living in your home.

BACKSPLASHES

Consider smaller backsplashes due to wall cabinets that are lower and easier to reach.

Use contrasting colors so it's easier to see.

Surface should be easy-to-clean and non-glare material.

FLOORING

Use smooth or lower threshold levels to avoid stumbles.

Consider a smooth, non-glare, slip-resistant surface, such as matte ceramic tile.

Contrasting colors and textures make different levels easier to see.

Do not use stone products—they require sealing every two to three years.

Go with a good quality, solid vinyl floor surface if tile would be too hard on the knees or back.

Do not use slippery rugs or put a pad underneath to make them secure.

Allow for a five foot space for turning around with ease (remove the island, if necessary).

APPLIANCE FIXTURES

Buttons and labels should be large enough to be easily read.

Control buttons should be on the front of the appliance and easy to reach.

Wheelchair space, if needed at appliances area, should be 30" x 48."

Choose appliances that are easy to clean.

Wall ovens versus range ovens:

> Wall ovens are easier to use than range ovens for placing heavy pots inside.
>
> Side-swing door is preferable.
>
> Appliances should it be raised from floor level for easier reach.
>
> Self-cleaning oven is preferable.

Controls and operating mechanisms should have a maximum high forward reach of 48" and a maximum low forward reach of 15."

Watch which way the door opens on a wall oven. A door that fully opens to the right or left will allow you to get closer to the oven to lift heavy pans out, whereas a drop-down door will keep you further away.

Refrigerator and freezer:

> Refrigerator should be side-by-side.
>
> Refrigerator drawers are a great option and need to be placed in base cabinets.
>
> Controls should be within arm's reach between 15" and 48" above the floor.
>
> Fresh food should be placed below 54."
>
> Refrigerator drawers for drinks are easy to reach.

Dishwasher:

> Dishwasher drawers are a great option and need to be placed in base cabinets.
>
> Raise the dishwasher a few inches above the countertop so it requires less bending.
>
> Push-button controls are easier to maneuver.
>
> Interior should be easy to load and unload.
>
> Controls should be within arms' reach between 15" and 48" above the floor.

Cook top or range:

- Electric is preferred over gas.

- It should include a downdraft feature that pulls heat away from the user.

- If a cook top or range with an overhead hood is chosen, make sure it includes a remote control so it's easy to use.

- It should include a hot-surface indicator light.

- Induction cook top prevent burns.

- Controls should be on the front panels, so you don't have to reach across hot burners.

- The controls are positioned within a forward reach of 15" — 48."

- It should be installed at various heights with knee space underneath for wheelchair access.

- Smooth top electric models allow easy pot movement and cleaning (our arms lose their strength and hand grips weaken as we age).

Microwave:

- Should be easy to reach even when you are seated.

- Microwave drawers are a great option and need to be placed in base cabinets.

- Controls should be within easy reach of 15" to 48."

PLUMBING FIXTURES

Single-lever faucets with pull-out sprayers are best.

Should be placed on the side of the sink for easier reach.

Motion-sensor faucets are preferable.

Instant hot water feature is best, but use with caution.

An under-mount sink is easier to clean and doesn't need to be maintained with caulk.

Consider two sinks, (a normal size and a small one), which allow for two cooks to work at the same time.

LIGHTING FIXTURES

Multiple sources of light should cover all areas and tasks, and prevent shadowed areas.

Increase bulb wattage and use dimmers with pre-set devices to allow for easier on/off operation and variable lighting intensity.

Rocker or touch light switches are easier to maneuver.

Add lighting under wall cabinets to provide good light on countertops—this also illuminates backsplashes, making them look like pieces of art.

Light the inside of wall cabinets to make contents easier to see.

Use automated lighting if your budget will allow for it.

Lighting above the wall cabinets creates a nice glow and also acts as night lights.

Motion sensors in the pantry help illuminate contents.

Lower switch plates for easy reach.

Raise wall outlets for easy reach.

Use ground-fault circuit interrupter plugs in wet areas to protect from severe electrical shocks.

HARDWARE FIXTURES

Cabinet hardware: Use pulls instead of knobs—they are easier to grab, which is especially helpful for people with arthritis.

Interior and exterior doors: Use lever handles—they are easier to grab and open when carrying groceries or other materials.

WALLS

Use light colors that brighten the kitchen.

Use paint that is easy to clean.

GLASS

Clear glass doors help to see what's inside.

FABRIC

Low maintenance, easy-to-wash material for seats, benches, and window treatments is best.

STORAGE

Lighting is installed in the pantry.

Shelves are adjustable or roll-out.

Doors are easy to open and will not obstruct a wheelchair.

WINDOWS

Many windows are installed to provide as much natural light as possible (a skylight is a great option).

Inside and outside finishes are low-maintenance.

Windows are installed lower than standard, or are taller windows with a lower sill height.

Hardware are easy to open and will not obstruct a wheelchair.

SAFETY

Install smoke and carbon monoxide detectors.

Make sure electrical cords are out of the flow of traffic.

Have an emergency alert or a video monitoring system installed.

HALLWAYS

Hallways should be at least 42" wide and well lit.

Rugs and floor runners should be skid-resistant and secured.

Unnecessary rugs and floor runners should be removed.

Hallways should be kept clutter-free.

HEATING, VENTILATION, AND AIR CONDITIONING

Units should be energy efficient.

Filters should be easily accessible.

Windows should be easy to open to allow fresh air into the house.

REDUCED MAINTENANCE AND CONVENIENCE FEATURES

Surfaces should be smooth and easy to clean—just be careful on a slippery floor.

Include a built-in recycling system.

Video phones should be installed.

A central vacuum system should be installed.

A pet feeding system should be built in.

An intercom system should be installed.

> Having a kitchen designed using Universal Design principles not only helps you or your parents stay in your home longer, it helps the house sell faster when that time comes. There is a big demand for Universally Designed homes in the future.

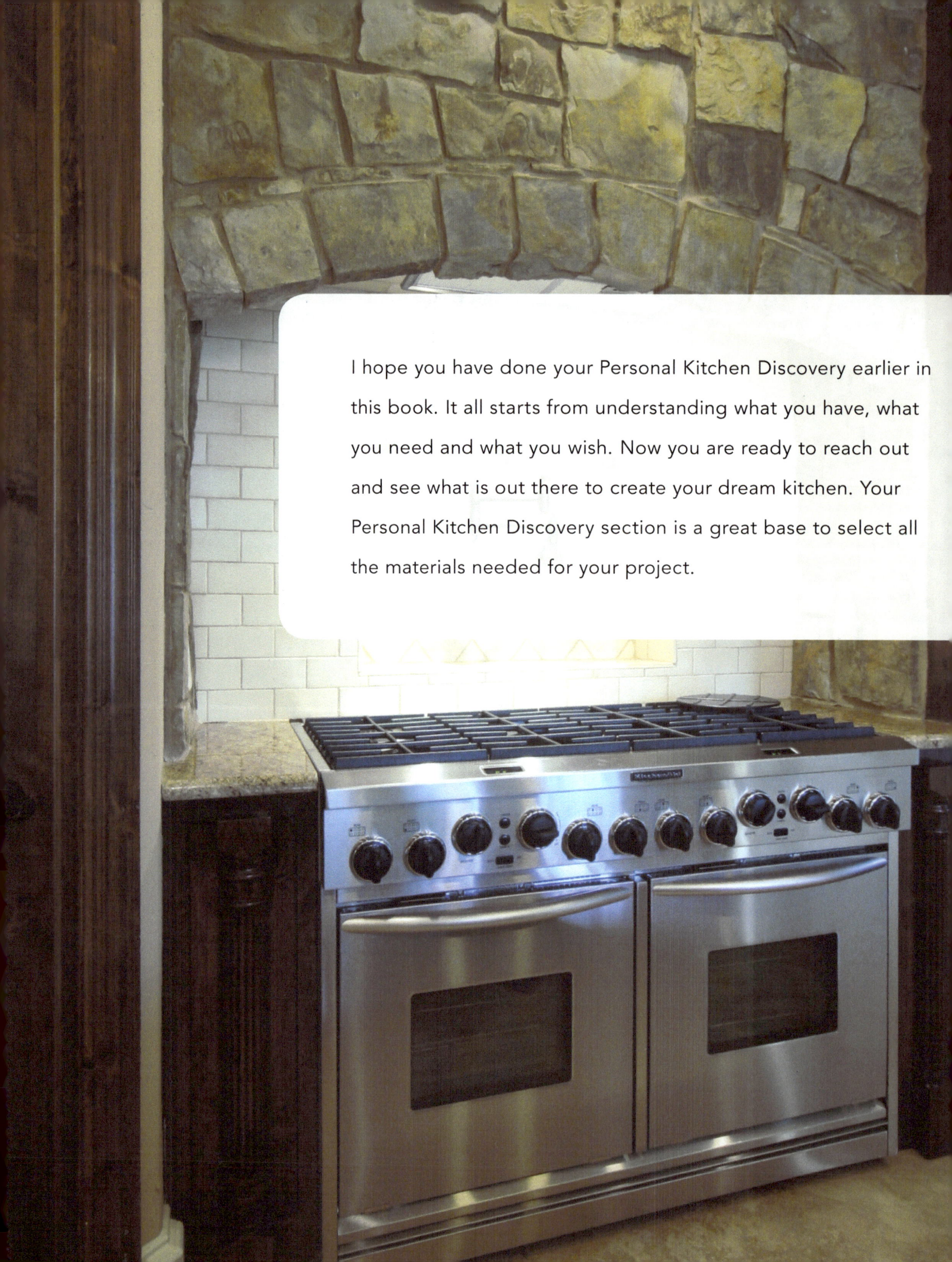

I hope you have done your Personal Kitchen Discovery earlier in this book. It all starts from understanding what you have, what you need and what you wish. Now you are ready to reach out and see what is out there to create your dream kitchen. Your Personal Kitchen Discovery section is a great base to select all the materials needed for your project.

Steps of Discovery of Material

STEP 1
Color

STEP 2
Metal

STEP 3
Architectural

STEP 4
Miscellaneous

BONUS:
Outside kitchen

CHAPTER FIVE

"Every designer has his/her own way of going about this process. I like to start with selecting the countertop. Then I follow with the cabinets if we will be using stock or existing cabinets, backsplash, flooring, walls, ceiling, trims, and doors—usually in that order."

Surround yourself with color that makes you feel happy, peaceful, or energized, depending on the mood you want to create. For some people, blue is relaxing and for others, red could also be relaxing.

As I explained in the "shopping" section of "Working with a designer," I choose the colors first when starting the material selection. I start with the countertop. Next, I do the cabinet color (if it is a custom line), then the backsplash and flooring, and finally, the paint color for the walls, ceiling, doors and trim. All of these colors should coordinate with the countertop or your existing material from the other room especially if it is an open concept.

> If working with existing or stock cabinets, start working with them first because they have fewer color choices than do countertops. Then I move to the metals — the appliances, plumbing fixtures, lighting fixtures, hardware fixtures, architectural and miscellaneous details.

We accomplish more by starting where we have the fewest choices, then matching all of the rest to that. Be sure to bring along a piece of existing material to make sure it matches the new material. Get samples of the new material as well, so you can keep matching as you go.

IMPORTANT: It is impossible to explain and provide pictures of every product available. If I did, this book would be hundreds and hundreds of pages long. I will provide an idea of what is out there and highly recommend that you go visit stores and browse the Internet. By doing that, you will also have an idea of what is new when the time comes to design your kitchen, and you won't depend on a book that cannot be updated.

STEP 1: Color

Countertops

Cabinets

Backsplash and floorings

Walls, ceiling, doors, and trims

COUNTERTOPS

Natural Countertop   Synthetic Countertop   Basic Countertop Edge Profile

Start by looking at the different materials. Touch them and ask about the maintenance. Each kind has its own pros and cons. I will list a few of the favorites here for you.

Don't be afraid to mix and match colors and materials on the countertop. It will allow you to create an eclectic look and personalize your space more. Using different colors helps to create interesting textures and balances. You can enjoy high-end materials, even if you are working on a tight budget, by using expensive materials on little areas, and then being more economical for the main area. Be careful when mixing and matching; you don't want the material to compete for your attention. For example, use a busy pattern with a solid color instead of with another pattern.

HERE A TWO CATEGORIES OF COUNTERTOPS. THERE ARE MORE CATEGORIES OF COUNTERTOPS THAT ARE NOT LISTED BELOW.

Natural	Synthetic
Granite, Marble, Travertine, Limestone, Onyx, soapstone and wood.	Quartz, Solid Surface, Glass and Recycle Glass, Concrete, Copper, Laminate and Tile.

NATURAL COUNTERTOP

If you decide to use a natural product, I recommend you look at those countertop slabs first-hand. Wear you walking shoes — some places require a lot of walking and you do not want to hurry the process. It is so fun to see all the different slabs and where they came from. Take time to browse around all of the big slabs. They are very impressive and very beautiful. It can be overwhelming at first, but look at what you are attracted to and make note of the names, the row where the slab you like is in case you want to come back to see it again. Then go through your list and go see them again. Narrow your choices down to 1, 2 and 3. The slab showroom will probably not be able to give you prices of the slabs because they only sell to fabricators, but they can give you rough ideas of the level or pricing for the slab you like. It is a great ideas to ask your designer what level of slab price has been budget for you. Also bring a flash light with you because sometimes the slabs are placed side by side and are hard to see the details, you may ask to have it pulled it out and placed where you can see it completely. Some showrooms will only show slab by appointment only. In the case, you may have to make an appointment to come back another time or call in before you get there. Make sure they have enough of the slab from the same lot for your countertop; otherwise it may not match well when it is put together in your kitchen. Some slabs, even with the same name, can differ a lot from one lot to another. Always keep in mind the best thing to do is to hand pick the one you want.

The slabs are available in two sizes — 2 cm and 3 cm (3 cm thickness is about 1 inch). I use the 3 cm for kitchen countertops because it will look like a bigger countertop.

Granite has many variations; some have more color and some have a more uniform look, some look spotty and some have more movement. The price of granite will be influenced by how rare the granite is and where it came from. You will need a professional to install your slab countertop — this is not a "do it yourself" project.

Don't forget to seal any natural stone countertop during the installation process. Regular maintenance will be required every two to five years, depending on the sealer used. Don't go cheap on the sealer; you won't save any money, and you will have to do it more often. Cheap sealer also may not protect as well. Use a revitalizer to both clean on a daily basis and to help reseal. This gives you more time before having to reseal again.

I don't recommend using marble, travertine, limestone, soapstone or onyx in a kitchen because these materials are too porous. It may look good, but you don't want to worry about staining your countertop. You probably have seen a white carrera marble countertop in magazine or models home, but I don't recommend it. What you see in a magazine doesn't mean it will be practical for your daily living.

Soapstone is beautiful by its simplicity. It won't burn if you set a hot pot or pan on it, but, it could stain if you don't regularly apply mineral oil. They also can be sanded down if scratched. Soapstone is best used in a place that isn't used much or for food, because it can stain or scratch.

You can save money by choosing a remnant slab piece of the stone. A remnant piece of slab is a "left over" from another job the fabricator has done, so you can buy a smaller piece for a smaller area of kitchen countertop, such as for an island, and save money by not having to pay for a whole slab. You can find remnants at the slab showroom at the fabricator shop. If you are looking for a specific slab, be sure to call them before going there — they might not have it.

Granite and marble can be finished in different ways: polished, brushed or honed. The polish will be soft and shiny; the brushed will be textured, and honed will be soft but not shiny.

Marble

Limestone

Granite

Granite

Granite

Wood

SYNTHETIC COUNTERTOPS

QUARTZ—is easy to maintain and doesn't require sealing maintenance. Quartz is stronger than granite, doesn't scratch or stain, and is available in many colors.

SOLID SURFACE—is easy to maintain and doesn't require sealing maintenance. Solid Surface can be repaired easily if scratched and you can choose a solid surface undermounted sink, and it will be seamless.

GLASS—glass countertops come in many colors and textures and are quite sturdy. Glass countertops can also be environmentally friendly if they are made from recycled glass and don't require sealing maintenance. Just be careful not to drop something heavy on them! Choosing a texture or patterned glass will help hide scratches; clear or solid colors will be less forgiving.

CONCRETE—concrete countertops are mixed and made to fit right at your house. They can be expensive and must be sealed, but they are heat and scratch-resistant and can look very unusual and unique, if that is your style. You may also insert deco pieces into concrete countertops, such as mosaic tile, metal or glass.

COPPER—the interesting feature about copper countertops is their anti-microbial aspect; supposedly, copper can kill 99.9% of bacteria within two hours. Copper countertops can easily be cleaned with soap and water. Copper is relatively soft, however, so these countertops are prone to scratching, and the color fades over time. Use for a small area or when you want to mix and match the countertop with something else.

ECONOMIC OPTIONS

CERAMIC TILE—ceramic tile is durable, fairly inexpensive, and easy to clean. You can also save more money if you install it yourself. Ceramic tile is available in many choices of style, color, size and price. Be aware of the grout maintenance; it can be very hard to keep the grout looking good. If you like this kind of a countertop, use the biggest tile you can (24" x 24" or 12" x 24"), and use the smallest grout joint possible. Don't get white or black colored grout—they will show every bit of dirt, and the white won't stay white. Think about the countertop edge; you might want to be creative with glass or stone mosaic, or go a safer route with the bullnose edge that matches the tile and can be purchased with the tile.

LAMINATE—Is the countertop that is the most affordable. It is commonly used in many homes because of its low cost, but has been criticized for not being very attractive. However, there are new designs that have the look of stone and are attractive. Laminate is available in several styles and finishes.

Keep in mind that granite, quartz and solid surface are great countertop materials for a heavy traffic area like a kitchen.

Quartz

Other Fun Countertops

We used to see a lot of 4" backsplash, which was made of the same material as the countertop. These days, I recommend using a different material and install the full height. I would not recommend a 4" backsplash in the same material as the countertop and then install tile above—it looks like an afterthought and would make your backsplash appear smaller. The only exception for me would be if you have a dramatic stone to make a big statement and use it in one backsplash area, like a cooktop or buffet area. There are so many different kinds of countertop to have fun with by mixing them. They come in different material like stone (travertine, marble, slate, onyx, limestone, glass, metal, etc.

> If you will be keeping the existing countertop and floor, and are lucky enough to have samples of them, be sure to take them with you when you go shopping for the rest of the materials.

COUNTERTOP ACCESSORY

If you have unused cabinet space in the corner, you might want to utilize that area by adding a countertop composter. They can be installed directly into the countertop and used to collect organic waste. It comes with a bucket that can be easily removed for cleaning.

BASIC COUNTERTOP EDGES PROFILE

Circle the edge profiles you like best. Be aware of sharp corners; always have them rounded to prevent injuries. And, of course, the more elaborate, the more expensive. Others edges profile are available, those five are the basic.

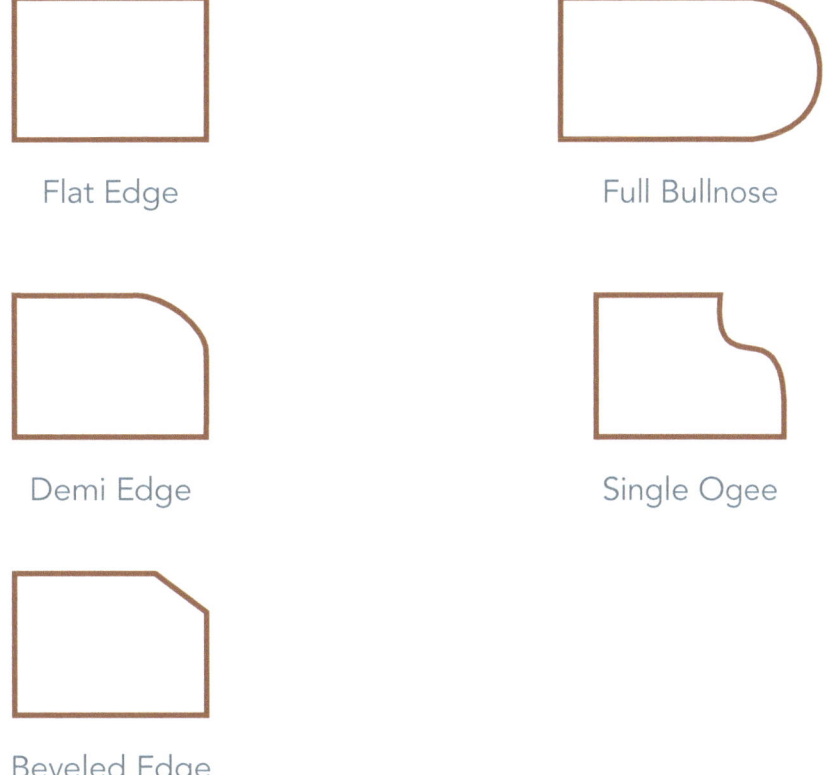

As you look through your catalogs and magazines, cut out the pictures of countertops that catch your eye and put them on the next few pages.

Do you like a busy or solid pattern?

Are you attracted by light or dark countertops?

Do you like mixing and use different materials together?

Don't forget to look at the Universal Design section for more on Countertops.

PICTURES OF COUNTERTOPS YOU LIKE:

PICTURES OF COUNTERTOPS YOU LIKE:

STEPS OF DISCOVERY OF MATERIAL

CABINETS

Refinishing cabinets　　Refacing cabinets　　Replacing with new cabinets

Construction　　Material　　Style

Color　　Accessories

You have options when remodeling your kitchen cabinets. You can replace, refinish or reface your cabinets. If you are satisfied with the layout of your existing cabinets, all you may need is to refresh their look with refinishing or refacing.

Always ask for a quote for painting, refacing or to replacing cabinets. You can be surprised with the price difference.

REFINISHING (PAINTING OR RESTAINING) CABINETS

Things to consider:

Gloss or semi-gloss finish.

Sprayed-on finish is recommended because the paint is applied more uniformly.

Keep in mind painted cabinets tend to accumulate grease and dust and could be more difficult to maintain. It is also at risk for peeling if the surface was not been properly prepared.

If you decide to paint, make sure you hire a painter who is knowledgeable on painting cabinets, not walls.

If you want to re-stain, be aware that you can't re-stain to a lighter color than the existing one. Since the stain penetrates the wood, it is impossible to stain to a lighter color.

Ask your painter for more information about refinishing your existing cabinets.

REFACING CABINETS

Refacing involves replacing the door and drawer fronts

You can change the color and style of your cabinets.

The process is done by covering the visible parts of the cabinet with veneer, which are easy to clean.

Ask a professional for more information.

REPLACING WITH NEW CABINETS

If you choose to replace your cabinets, know that this decision will influence the style of your kitchen and is a big part of your budget. Here are some things to keep in mind when deciding on your cabinets:

Custom cabinets are made to the specifications of a particular order. The more customized your cabinets, the more expensive they will be, just as a specially-ordered piece of furniture would be more expensive than ordering from the floor. There is sometimes a fine line between custom and stock cabinetry.

Many large custom manufacturers offer a wide range of standard sizes and finishes, which can be modified by altering size, customizing finishes or colors, changing the configurations, and adding accessories. When changes are made to stock cabinets, they are then considered custom cabinets and will cost more.

Stock cabinets are manufactured in standard sizes before orders are placed. The manufacturer keeps them in inventory until someone orders them. Custom cabinets will take more time to fabricate than stock cabinets.

The decision for stock or custom cabinets will depend on your budget and project time frame. Make sure the fabrication and delivery of the cabinets fit the time frame of your renovation.

The trims are important too. The crown and chair rail moldings placed above and below your wall cabinets come in different styles and different sizes. You can also have deco pieces like fluted column. Placing a little molding below the wall cabinets will hide the light fixtures.

Think, too, about the style, shape, and color for your doors, drawers, and trims, and if you want them to be painted or stained in a light or dark color. One cabinet manufacturer may offer hundreds of door styles in an endless array of finishes.

When you think about kitchen cabinets, think of Lego's' blocks. Cabinets are individual pieces that join together to fill the wall or island where you want cabinets. A designer will help you create the cabinet layout that fits your lifestyle. Don't forget to use the zones we talked about earlier in chapter 3 of this book.

Work with a designer for the layout of your cabinets to make sure it is functional to your needs.

CONSTRUCTION

There are four components to a cabinet:

Cabinet boxes — are made of plywood or the most common material — engineered wood. The exterior will be made of the material you want to see.

Drawers — are stronger when doweled or dovetailed.

Drawer glides — I recommend a full extension glide, but the standard 3/4 extension is okay too.

Shelves — make sure they are adjustable instead of fixed. Roll-out shelves are very convenient and make it easier to see what is on the shelf.

Hinges — can be exposed, decorative, or fully concealed, as well as adjustable and self-closing.

Overlay — full overlay (when cabinet doors completely cover the cabinet box), or standard (the doors are smaller than the box).

> Be careful with all the fancy details like big crown molding, corbel or pillars. They will add cost to your cabinets quickly. If the budget allows it and it is your style, go ahead and have fun with it.

MATERIAL

Wood

Pay attention to the grain of the wood, because it has to match the style you want to achieve. For example, too much wood grain will not fit with a modern style, but it would be great for a rustic style.

KINDS OF WOOD

Oak

Hickory

Painted Wood

Maple

Cherry

Maple with glaze

Thermafoil (laminate) — won't fade or discolor, is cheaper, and can be cleaned with soap and water.

There are different materials you can choose for door inserts. Examples are: wood, glass, copper or stainless steel, chicken wire etc. Use your imagination and always make sure it is easy to clean. See below for glass examples.

STYLE

The cabinet style and color will influence the style of your kitchen.

There are many, many door shapes and styles to consider. Just find the shape and materials that add to your style. For instance, a slab door might look nice if your style is sharp and defined, such as with stainless steel. If you like ornate and decorative better, choose something like a raised panel door.

Be aware of the style of your home. You don't want to do a contemporary style kitchen in a country house. But if you do not intend to sell soon, you can consider mixing styles — this is what we call "eclectic". I explained this in step 3 of "How do you find your style?"

SLAB — sleek and simple.

RAISED PANEL — raised pieces of lumber, usually between ½" and ¾" thick with routed edges, give the cabinet an elegant look.

RECESSED PANEL — gives the cabinet a picture-frame look and country feeling.

CURVED PANEL—raised panel with a gentle arch at the top.

CATHEDRAL PANEL—raised or recessed panel with a cathedral arch at the top.

BEADBOARD PANEL—recessed panel with beadboard elements.

COLOR

When choosing the colors, think about your kitchen lifestyle. Light colors will show smudges and dirt, but dust won't be noticed as easily.

Be careful on wood color—they can have a base or undertone color of yellow or gold, pink or red, or green (like all other colored material, such as countertops or tile). It needs to have the same base or undertone color to be harmonious. Also, when working with a custom stain color, you should try a sample on the wood you want to use. The same stain color will not give a different color on different woods because of their undertones.

You can also mix the color of cabinets. For example, the island can be a different color than the rest of the cabinets. The hood and base of the cook top can be the same color and the rest another color. Don't be afraid to mix colors, but make sure the colors are relatively harmonious.

Paint—offers a smooth, uniform consistency.

Painted cabinets can be glazed; glazed cabinets will look worn and aged. A watered down layer of a different paint color is applied to the surface of the cabinet.

Stain—adds a rich look to the wood and brings out the grain. They can be stained a dark or light color. Like painted cabinets, they can be glazed too.

ACCESSORIES

Here are lots of possibilities and decisions when it comes to the accessories. When the accessories need to be place inside your cabinets you need to be sure it fit the space. They need to be planned at the cabinet layout phase. Here are some things to consider:

A pull-out for spices below a corbel. Make sure you install one on each side of the cooktop for symmetry.

A pull-out shelf by your stove for easy movement of heavy pots and pans

Open shelves can add style to your décor and display your collections or cookbooks. They can be placed on wall or base cabinets.

Racks for your favorite plate and little drawers.

Lazy susan or pull-out shelves for those inaccessible corners.

Divider for the cutlery so everything stays in place when you open the drawer.

Wine bottle cubes, shelves, and appliances storage.

Pantry with easy reach.

Trash and recycle bins under the sink so you don't spill on the floor on your way to the trash can.

Tilt-down sponge tray

Cutlery dividers

Tray dividers for your cookie sheets

Adjustable shelving

Pull-up mixer shelf

> An appliance garage sits on the countertop and is perfect to hide the small appliances that we use every day, but unclutters the countertop—you will love that. Make sure you have enough plugs for all the small appliances and good lighting.

Paste your pictures of the cabinet wood, color, or style on the next pages: (You may search accessories on the internet to find more ideas, but be careful because not all the stock cabinets offer them). The more expensive the line, the more accessory choices you may have.

Don't forget to look at the Universal Design section of the book for more ideas on Cabinets.

PICTURES OF THE CABINET WOOD, COLOR, OR STYLE YOU LIKE:

PICTURES OF CABINET ACCESSORIES YOU LIKE:

STEPS OF DISCOVERY OF MATERIAL

BACKSPLASH

Backsplashes are fun. The stores always have new products, so I recommend you visit your local tile store to see what has come in. Don't forget to take pictures so you can put the ones you like in this book!

Pay special attention to the space above your cook top or range. Usually there is a taller space where something special could be created, such as a mural. If you have a vent microwave above the range or cooktop, you will have less space available.

Or you can have fun and install the mosaic up to the ceiling, to give a tall effect.

Don't forget the sides of your backsplash—sometimes there is a sharp edge because they had to cut the tile to fit the space. The sides should not have a sharp cut edge. You can apply a clean grout line that will cover the entire side, or a small stone molding pieces or a bullnose that match the tile.

For the rest of the backsplash, you can use borders and change the material below and underneath.

ECONOMIC OPTIONS

You can use inserts or decos in your backsplash. Keep in mind that a border will cost more than deco because you buy them by pieces, like 2x6, 3x8, 4x12 ect.and the pieces itself is not always economical. An economic way of creating drama is to buy sheets of mosaic and cut them in border shapes or deco shapes. The mosaic can be made of stone, glass, metal, or ceramic tile and in several sizes. Also, just insert deco pieces of 1x1, 2x2, 3x3 up to 8x8 randomly or strategically, made of different material.

Sizes   Patterns   Materials   Grout   Sealer for grout   Sealer for stone

SIZES

From ½" x ½" up to 3" x 3" mosaics, 3" x 6", 4" x 4", 6" x 6", 4" x 8", 8" x 8", 8" x 16", and small and large harlequin.

PATTERNS

Square, diagonal, brick, multi sizes, pin wheel, herringbone, and others.

You can search for tile patterns on the internet to see more options. Just make sure the tile you like has the size or sizes required to achieve the pattern.

Diagonal layout

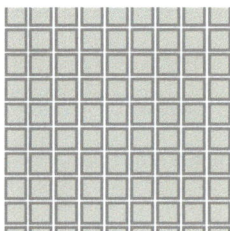

Square layout

Brick layout

Pin wheel or hopscotch layout

Herringbone layout

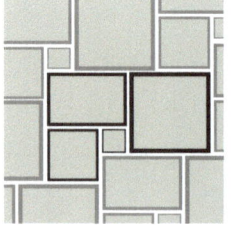

Multi size layout

MATERIAL

Some commonly used materials are: Stone, glass, glazed ceramic, metal like stainless steel, copper, bronze and even clear plastic glass sheet that you can decorate behind all kind of flat material. And don't forget, you can mix material.

STONE TILE

Sizes range from ½" x ½" mosaic to 12" x 12" tile, and everything in between. Stone tile comes in travertine, marble, onyx, granite, and slate. Stone tile requires regular sealing. Here are some pictures of stone tile samples:

GLASS TILE

Sizes range from ½" x ½" mosaic to 8" x 8" tile. You can also find mesh mixed with glass and stone tile. Here are some examples:

CERAMIC GLAZE TILE

Sizes range from ½" x ½" mosaic to 8" x 8". Sometimes you can find 12" x 12" tile. If you tile the backsplash and end with an open wall, you will have to watch how you hide the unfinished side of the tile. Bullnose or pencil tile work well for this. Here are some samples of the ceramic glaze tile:

METAL

Available in sheets or tile. The metals finished are stainless steel, copper, bronze, chrome, brushed nickel.

MIXED MATERIAL

Have fun and mix materials on your backsplash. Mix stone and glass, stone and ceramic tile, or stainless steel and glass; the combinations are endless. Be careful of the thickness of the material when placing them side by side; it is best to have similar thicknesses.

GROUT

The grout is important. I like to blend it with the tile so it isn't emphasized. But if you like contrast, the grout can help to achieve that. If you choose a stone tile with holes, be aware that the grout will set in every hole. If you have a chipped side tile you'll see more grout than the initial joint size, you grout will look bigger. Also, be very careful with black grout; it is very difficult to clean during installation. You should also seal all light grout color.

The industry is working on fabricating more stain resistant grout. Check with your local tile store to see what is new and see if other people like it before you buy.

SEALER FOR GROUT

Don't forget to seal your grout. I recommend sealing the grout as soon as the job is done and reseal about every three years, depending on how much traffic you have. Never seal a glaze tile; it will peel up like nail polish, and you will need to strip the entire floor. Please don't go there—it is a nightmare.

SEALER FOR STONE

Natural stone will require sealer. You may choose a clear sealer, which will not change the color, or an enhancer sealer which will intensify the existing color and make it more colorful. The quality of the sealers is the same—it is just the final look that changes.

Seal your stone backsplash before grouting. This will make cleaning a lot easier because the stone is porous. Reseal the stone as well as the grout afterwards.

> Don't forget to look at the Universal Design section of the book for more ideas on backsplashes.

PICTURES OF BACKSPLASHES YOU LIKE:

STEPS OF DISCOVERY OF MATERIAL

FLOORING

Flooring comes in many choices. Be careful of the thicknesses where different flooring meets -you don't want to trip on it.

Here are some explanations of the five most popular floorings:

Ceramic tile   Grout   Sealer for grout   Hardwood
Laminate   Natural stone   Sealer for stone   Vinyl

CERAMIC TILE

This tile is easy to maintain. Go with the larger tile (minimum 18" x 18") for a more updated look, and don't be afraid to mix sizes and colors.

Sizes available: 18" x 18", 20" x 20", 12" x 18", and multi-sizes. Patterns: Square, diagonal, brick, multi-sizes, pin wheel, herringbone, and others. Make sure the tile you like has all of the sizes that the pattern requires.

Types of ceramic tile: Red body, glaze porcelain, and through-body porcelain. I recommend the glaze porcelain; it is stronger a stronger body.

You will probably not like the look of ceramic tile after you have looked at real stone -the ceramic tile will look fake. But if you don't want to do regular maintenance, resist the temptation to buy real stone. There are ceramic tiles available now that imitate the look of real stone and wood quite well.

NEVER put carpet in the kitchen.

GROUT

The grout is important. As with the backsplash, the grout can either be blended or contrasted, but be careful with the contrasted color, with the stone tile with holes it will show all the holes. Be sure to keep the grout line small and know that white grout stains

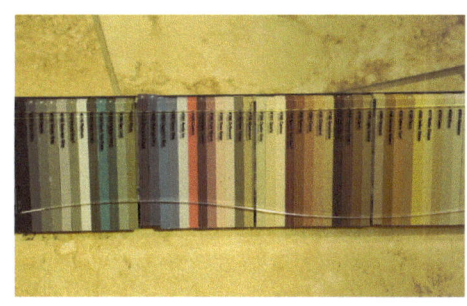

easily. If you have a chipped side tile you'll see more grout than the initial joint size, and your grout will look bigger. Also, be very careful with black grout; it is very difficult to clean during installation

SEALER FOR GROUT

Don't forget to seal your grout. I recommend sealing the grout as soon as the job is done and reseal about every three years, depending on how much traffic you have. Never seal a glaze tile; it will peel up like nail polish, and you will need to strip the entire floor. Please don't go there—it is a nightmare.

HARDWOOD

Comes in solid or engineering wood floor.

SOLID WOOD—be careful because it's thicker than other floor material. It is usually apply when you are building a new home; the builder will make sure the height between other floors and how high to set the door will work. They also will have to stain the wood in the house. Also it is recommended to let the flooring set in the house for a couple days so it will adjust to the temperature. Otherwise it may change size a little after you have installed it.

ENGINEERING WOOD—is the best for remodeling. It comes already stained and the thickness is more compatible with the other floorings.

This is a pretty choice, but be very careful about using it in a kitchen. I have had to replace wood floors because the dishwasher or fridge leaked. I know hardwood floors are better quality than they used to be and some people have no problem with it, but I would still be careful. If you really like the wood look, there is tile available that looks just like wood. Nothing can replace the real warmth of wood, so if it is something you just have to have, go for it, but at least you will know what to expect. Also, the darker the color and less grain in the wood, the more dirt will show.

Engineering wood floor

LAMINATE

This flooring will look like real wood but will be much easier to maintain. Be aware of the hollow sound—make sure you are using a good pad underneath it.

NATURAL STONE

This is stone such as travertine, marble, or slate. These floors look very nice but they are also hard to maintain. You don't want to worry about it chipping every time someone drops something on the floor. Be sure to seal your stone flooring to make cleaning a lot easier because the stone is so porous.

No ceramic tile will look as beautiful after you have seen real stone. If you absolute must have stone, at least you will know what to expect.

SEALER FOR STONE

As mentioned in the backsplash/grout section, natural stone will require sealer. You may choose a clear sealer, which will not change the color, or an enhancer sealer which will intensify the existing color and make it more colorful. The quality of the sealers is the same—it is just the final look that changes.

The advantage of having a stone floor is you can seal the stone tile and the grout all together, so the application is faster.

Seal your stone floor before grouting. This will make cleaning a lot easier because the stone is porous. Reseal the stone as well as the grout afterwards.

> Think twice before choosing stone for your floor if you have kids and/or pets, it will get more abuse.

VINYL

Vinyl comes in a roll, or tiles of 12" x 12" or 18" x 18". The vinyl does a pretty good job of mimicking the look of real stone and wood.

> Don't forget to look at the Universal Design section of the book for more ideas on Flooring.

PICTURES OF FLOOR STYLE AND SIZES YOU LIKE:

PICTURES OF FLOOR STYLE AND SIZES YOU LIKE:

STEPS OF DISCOVERY OF MATERIAL

WALLS, CEILINGS, DOORS AND TRIMS

This section is pretty self-explanatory. Put your samples on the next pages.

Paint   Stain   Wallpaper

PAINT

Some hints and tips:

Because there are so many choices, the paint color should be your last decision. Don't forget to look at the adjacent room wall color if it is an open concept kitchen.

We usually choose a paint color for the ceiling, walls, trims, and doors. If your ceiling is more than 10 square feet, you may use the color of

your wall if it's a light color. If your ceiling is less than ten square feet, I would use white, antique white or light beige, or a lighter color of the sample swatch.

Why is paint one of the hardest colors to choose? Because after applying it, it changes color depending on the light (natural, halogen, or fluorescent) and what it is surrounded by. I chose a beige color for a client's dining room and for some reason two of the beige walls had a pink tint to it and we figured out later that it was the red brick of an exterior wall that was reflecting through the window.

Always paint a 24" x 48" sample on the wall, or paint a board that you can move around, so you can look at the paint color on different walls and at different times of the day using natural and artificial light.

Should you use latex or oil paint? Latex paint is easier to apply and emits fewer odors than the oil –based, dries quickly, and can be cleaned up using soap and water. Oil-based paints is slow to dry, and needs to be cleaned with thinner or other solvents.

There is also a paint which is odorless. It costs a little more, but if you have problem with to strong smells, it may be worth the extra money, it is also good for the environment.

Paint finishes — this decision is based on the look you want:

> Flat offers a matte appearance that softens a room, and are good to use on ceilings.
>
> Satin paints are good for hallways and woodwork because they are very easy to clean.
>
> Semi-gloss paints are used in areas that are cleaned very frequently, such as kitchens and trims.
>
> Gloss is very hard and shiny, and is best used on wood trims and cabinets.

STAIN

Used for cabinets, trims, windows, and doors. Make sure your painters know how to stain wood and prepare the surface properly, otherwise you might not like the finished look. Ask to get a sample of the wood you will be using for your cabinets.

The color of the stain will change depending of what kind of wood you apply it to. You need to try a sample on the wood you will be using.

WALLPAPERS

This choice will depend on the look you are going for. Some things to remember:

> There are wall coverings available that have guarantees for being easy to install and remove. Some are not pre-pasted so you will need to follow the manufacturer's recommendation in order to apply it properly.
>
> Vinyls that are paper-backed, solid, and fabric-backed are very durable, so they are good to use in rooms with lots of traffic, such as a kitchen. Vinyl coated wallpaper also looks very elegant.

Create the Kitchen of a lifetime

Most wallpaper can be easily cleaned.

You might want to plan ahead in case you ever decide to remove the wallpaper. There are two kinds available now—peelable and strippable. Peelable wallpaper easily pulls off the wall; just the top layer is removed, leaving a plain layer which can be removed with soap and water. Strippable wallpaper pulls off completely, as long as the wall has been properly prepared in the first place, by using the manufacturer's instructions.

Don't forget to look at the Universal Design section of the book for more ideas on walls.

YOU CAN PASTE YOUR PAINT SAMPLES HERE:

PAINT SAMPLES:

STEPS OF DISCOVERY OF MATERIAL

145

STAIN SAMPLES:

Create the Kitchen of a lifetime

WALLPAPER SAMPLES:

STEPS OF DISCOVERY OF MATERIAL

"Don't forget to choose your appliances before ordering your cabinets. The cabinet maker will need to know the dimensions of your appliances in order to build the cabinets around them".

STEP 2: Metal

Appliances fixtures

Plumbing fixtures

Lighting fixtures

Hardware

APPLIANCE FIXTURES

Colors | Wood Paneled | Other Colors | Refrigerators | Ice Makers | Freezers

Wine Refrigerators | Ranges | Wall Ovens | Cooktops | Warming Drawers | Microwave Ovens

Speed Convection Cooking Ovens | Venting Systems and Hoods | Dishwashers | Coffee Machine | Trash Compactors

Thinking ahead about your appliances will help plan for the right locations of the electrical outlets, especially those requiring more wattage such as the oven and range. Remember, too, to consider the water supply to your refrigerator and dishwasher.

When replacing appliances and keeping the existing cabinets make sure the sizes of the new appliances will fit in the existing cabinets.

Make sure the oven, refrigerator, and dishwasher doors are not blocked by anything when you want to open them. Also, if your refrigerator is against a wall, add a tall "filler" between the refrigerator and the wall, so you can open the door wide enough to pull out the drawers inside.

If you kitchen has the room, you can have 2 of the same appliances. Examples are a regular refrigerator and a smaller one for beverages, or having two drawer dishwashers instead of regular one.

If you start from scratch, get all the appliances in the same color. If you have to deal with existing ones and like the color match the new ones to it. If you don't like the existing ones, get the new ones with the color you like and, when changing the older appliances, choose the new color you like will be.

Do you like smooth-top ranges? Side-by-side refrigerator and freezer? Here is the spot for you to put pictures of appliances you like. Because there are so many choices, I didn't include pictures for all of this section, but you can easily find pictures on the Internet if you want to know more about any of the appliances, or visit the appliance stores near you. They are stocked with the newest appliances and sometimes it's best to see them in person.

COLORS

Stainless steel

Black

White

Appliances come in several colors. The most popular are stainless steel, black, and white. The stainless steel color may vary from one brand to the other. Which color do you like most?

WOOD PANELED

Wine refrigerator

Fridge

They are designed to match your cabinets.

Dishwasher

OTHER COLORS

Be careful, as they can be very trendy and go out of style quicker.

REFRIGERATORS

Lots of choices some have a water dispenser or come without it. If you choose to have water dispenser or ice maker, be sure you have access to water. They also come built in, either inserted inside the cabinet, or free-standing with the sides finished. Which do you like most? You can also buy a regular size refrigerator and frame it with cabinet panels on both sides so it will look like a built-in, but costs less.

Side-by-side refrigerator

Bottom freezer refrigerator

With glass door and bottom freezer refrigerator

One door refrigerator

Upper freezer refrigerator

STEPS OF DISCOVERY OF MATERIAL

Refrigerator drawer

Create the Kitchen of a lifetime

154

PICTURES OF REFRIGERATORS YOU LIKE OR MARK THE ONE YOU LIKE ON THE PREVIOUS PAGE:

STEPS OF DISCOVERY OF MATERIAL

ICE MAKERS

They come with different sizes of ice and will need water access. Which do you prefer?

PICTURES OF ICE MAKERS YOU LIKE OR WHAT SIZE OF ICE I LIKE:

FREEZERS

Come as chest freezers or upright freezers. Which do you prefer?

PICTURES OF FREEZERS YOU LIKE:

STEPS OF DISCOVERY OF MATERIAL

WINE REFRIGERATORS

This appliance comes in countertop height or as a tall unit like in the picture below. It might not be a necessity, but they sure are nice to have if you are a wine lover.

PICTURES OF WINE REFRIGERATORS YOU LIKE:

RANGES

Any preferences? Remember that electric is recommended for Universal Design. Make sure you home has access to a gas line if you prefer gas.

Gas—free-standing

Gas—slide-in

Gas- slide-in double oven

Electric—free-standing

Electric—slide-in

If you want gas appliances and you have electrical appliances right now make sure you have access to a gas line. It can come from another room of the house like your fireplace or you may need to get access to your home from the outside. Either way you will add expenses to the budget.

PICTURES OF RANGES YOU LIKE OR MARK ONE ABOVE:

STEPS OF DISCOVERY OF MATERIAL

WALL OVENS

Deciding between a free-standing range, a stove and oven combination, or a wall oven is no easy task. The benefits of a wall oven are that it provides a space below your cooktop for big drawers to place your pots and pans. Wall ovens, like ranges, are electric or gas. Which would you like to have?

Single-double wall oven

Double wall oven

Gas- slide-in double ovenTriple appliances: microwave, oven, warming drawer combination

PICTURES OF WALL OVENS YOU LIKE OR MARK A PREVIOUS ONE:

STEPS OF DISCOVERY OF MATERIAL

COOKTOPS

Which do you prefer?

Gas cooktops

Electric glass cooktops

Coil electric cooktops

PICTURES OF COOKTOPS YOU LIKE OR MARK A PREVIOUS ONE:

STEPS OF DISCOVERY OF MATERIAL

WARMING DRAWERS

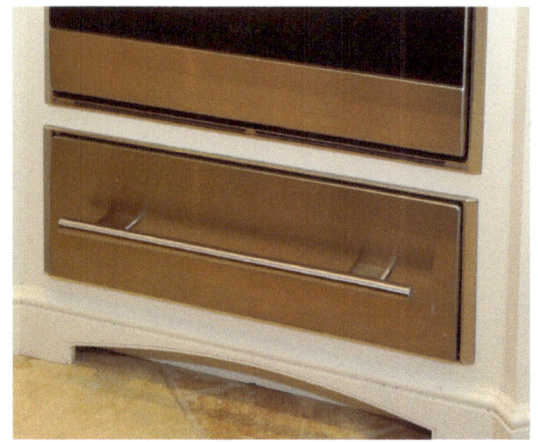

A warming drawer is a special drawer in your oven. It's often located at the bottom of the oven or in the base cabinet. It is used to warm plates or bread, or finish cooking a food item while the oven is used to bake something else. It is a great option if you have a bigger family, love to entertain or to keep a family member's food warm if they weren't able to have dinner with the rest of the family.

PICTURES OF WARMING DRAWER YOU LIKE:

MICROWAVE OVENS

Over-the-range microwave

Built-in microwave oven

Countertop microwave oven can also be mounting on wall cabinets to save countertop space.

Microwave drawer

PICTURES OF MICROWAVE OVENS YOU LIKE OR MARK ONE ABOVE:

SPEED CONVECTION COOKING OVENS

Speed-cooking ovens combine the speed of the microwave with the food quality of your regular oven. Meats, potatoes, and baked goods cook with the speed of the microwave but look like they've come out of your radiant heat oven. It's a perfect solution for today's fast-paced world.

Speed-cooking wall ovens

PICTURES OF SPEED-COOKING OVENS YOU LIKE OR MARK ONE ABOVE:

VENTING SYSTEMS AND HOODS

Help remove heat, moisture, and odors from the house after cooking. Be sure to choose a hood that is as wide as your range top in order for it to be as effective as possible. They come in standard or a more "designer" look. They can hide

behind other material or be visible. The surrounding material could be stone, wood, cooper, or tile. They make a beautiful stainless steel look too. The vent can be included with the microwave and we call this microwave/vent.

Microwave with ventilation.

STEPS OF DISCOVERY OF MATERIAL

PICTURES OF VENTING SYSTEMS AND HOODS YOU LIKE OR MARK ONE ABOVE:

DISHWASHERS

Dishwashers are built-in or portable, and each kind has their own advantages. Which most complements your lifestyle? Stainless steel, black, and white are the most popular colors.

They also come in a drawer format. They are awesome as they use less water and are easier to access.

Be careful on trendy color. They are more expensive and hard to match. You may also get tired of it quickly.

PICTURES OF DISHWASHERS YOU LIKE OR MARK ONE ABOVE:

COFFEE MACHINE

A design statement as well as built-in convenience. They can be placed on a countertop like the picture below or built in inside a tall unit. Be careful not to place it too high —it will be hard to see inside your cup.

Some coffee machines require plumbing in the wall to have instant water and others will need to be filled by adding water to the reservoir.

It is a great luxury appliance to have if you are a coffee lover.

PICTURES AND NOTES ABOUT COFFEE MACHINES:

TRASH COMPACTORS

Things to consider:

How easy is it to operate?

Does it include a filter and fan to control odors?

How well does it compact the trash?

Don't forget to look at the Universal Design section of the book for more ideas on Appliances fixtures.

TRASH COMPACTOR NOTES:

_____
_____
_____
_____
_____
_____
_____
_____
_____
_____
_____
_____
_____
_____
_____
_____

PLUMBING FIXTURES

| Faucets | Color | Sprayer or not | Spout height | Handles | Speciality Faucets |
| Soap Dispenser | Basin Sinks | Basin Sink Sizes | Basin Sink Styles | Basin Sink Finishes: | Garbage disposal |

If you can keep the plumbing in the same place as it is now, you will save money and be able to spend it on other things you like. If your plumbing is in a concrete slab, the concrete will need to be removed in order to redo the pipe in the new location. If you're lucky, your pipes will be located on the walls or on a regular wood floor structure but beware if you have a concrete slab. The cost for moving the pipe will be more expensive because you will have to jack out the concrete and fill it back in if you have a concrete slab. It is a lot easier and less expensive when you can access to your plumbing via a basement or pier beam foundation.

If you are building a new house, you start from scratch. Be creative when deciding where to put your sink(s). Would you like it to be in a corner or on a peninsula or in front of a window? Some people may get two sinks; a standard size and a smaller one because others are helping with cooking.

FAUCETS

COLOR

They come in chrome, pewter, brush nickel, satin, bronze, copper, black etc.

If you are remodeling your kitchen from scratch, get all the same finishes for your plumbing, lighting, appliances and appliances fixtures.

SPRAYER OR NOT

Pull-out or pull-down spray faucet—the spout pulls out of the faucet so you can easily control where the water goes. This type of faucet lets you control the water flow by stream or spray.

Photographs Courtesy of Kohler Co

Faucet with side spray—the spray can be on the left or the right side of the faucet, depending upon your needs.

Photographs Courtesy of Kohler Co

Faucet without side spray—for those who don't want the spray option.

Photographs Courtesy of Kohler Co

SPOUT HEIGHT

High-arch spout—lots of room under the faucet to wash pots and pans. These faucets range from 6" to 10" high.

Photographs Courtesy of Kohler Co

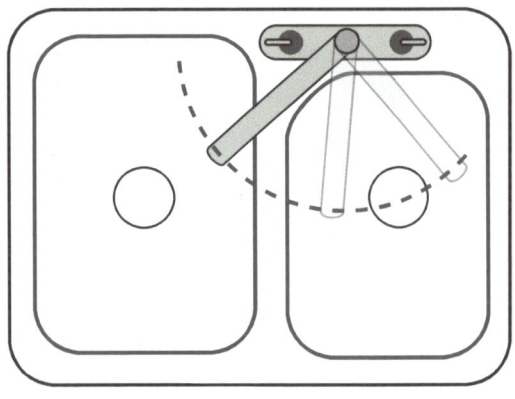

Spout reach—the water needs to reach the center of your sink, whether it's coming from your faucet or your sprayer. Be sure to think about both. If you have two sink basins, you should get a swivel faucet so you can reach both of them.

Photographs Courtesy of Kohler Co

HANDLES

Single-handled faucets turn to the left or right for hot or cold water. They also control the water flow. These faucets are good for using one hand, which complies with the Americans with Disabilities Act requirements.

Photographs Courtesy of Kohler Co

Two handles, one for hot and one for cold, are mixed to achieve the correct water temperature. You just need to pick the look you prefer for your kitchen, according to your style and your lifestyle.

Photographs Courtesy of Kohler Co

Handle styles—depend on the look you are going for in your kitchen. Choose the one that fits best. Blade and lever-type handles are the easiest to grab and turn.

Photographs Courtesy of Kohler Co

HINTS AND TIPS:

Make sure you choose a faucet that works with the sink you will be using.

Decide if you want your faucet to be sink-mounted or wall-mounted. If you want a sink-mounted faucet, you should count the number of holes in the sink and choose a faucet that can be used with them, unless you use an under-mount sink.

MORE INFORMATION ABOUT THE HOLES IN A SINK OR ON COUNTERTOP:

One hole—you'll need to use a faucet that has the handles on the base.

Two holes—you can use a one-piece faucet with individual handles, or you can use the second hole for a spray or soap dispenser.

Three holes—this would be for a faucet with separate handles on either side. Sometimes a faucet used in a single hole has a decorative base that would cover the extra holes in the sink.

Four holes—you can have a two-handle faucet, spray, and soap dispenser.

SPECIALTY FAUCETS

Hot and cold water filter dispensers are great for instant hot water for tea, hot chocolate or instant coffee and also cold drinking water.

Pot filler

SOAP DISPENSER

Soap dispenser has different metal color like the faucets. Make sure you get the same color as your faucet –it will be a cleaner look than the plastic soap bottle.

WHICH FAUCETS DO YOU LIKE? PUT YOUR PICTURES OF THEM HERE, OR MARK THE EXAMPLES ON THE PREVIOUS PAGES

WHICH FAUCETS DO YOU LIKE? PUT YOUR PICTURES OF THEM HERE, OR MARK THE EXAMPLES ON THE PREVIOUS PAGES

BASIN SINKS

How do you decide on a basin? Here are some ideas that might help:

If you use a dishwasher, you might prefer a sink with a large single basin. They are a bit smaller than a standard basin and you don't need to juggle your dishes over the divider.

If you have a large kitchen, you might want a second sink with a single basin in an island. This helps to make a second work area, which is handy when you have lots of guests over and everybody wants to help.

If you hand-wash your dishes, you would probably want your sink to have two or three basins. If you wash lots of pans, find a basin that is wider than standard and about 9" — 10" deep. The third basin could be where your disposal is located and is handy for scraping food directly into the sink.

Standard sinks are usually double basins, 33" x 22", and fit in cabinets that are 36" x 24"

Triple basin sinks are larger than standard size.

Make sure your under-mount sink is not bigger than your sink cabinet.

Be careful with black porcelain sinks. They look great, but they are very hard to keep clean because they may show every spot of water. The black granite composite sink is a great option.

You will need to have selected your sink and send it to the fabricator before they can fabricate your countertop unless you have a drop in sink, which can be cut on the job site. Otherwise they will have to cut the hole and polish the edge at the shop.

BASIN SINK SIZES:

SINGLE-BASIN SINKS

DOUBLE-BASIN SINK

TRIPLE-BASIN SINK

FUN SINKS

BASIN SINK STYLES:

UNDER-COUNTER SINKS—these are installed under the counter and are usually used with countertops such as granite, marble, or limestone. These are becoming more popular; clean-up is very easy because there is no rim. Installation is simple because the sink fits onto the base cabinet.

STEPS OF DISCOVERY OF MATERIAL

SELF RIMMING—The rim supports the sink on the countertop. Clips and bolts under the counter hold it in place. The faucet can be installed directly on the sink or on a ledge along the back.

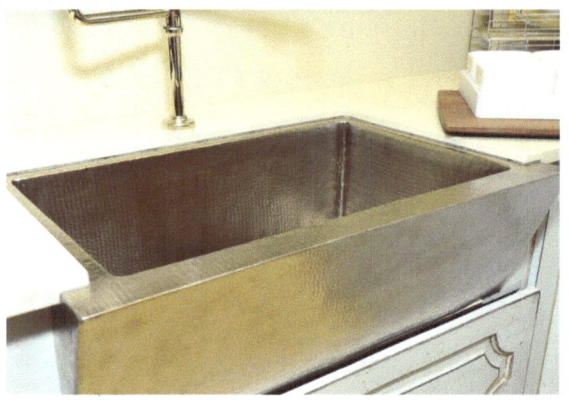 

APRON-FRONT—also known as a "farmhouse" sink. I recommend that you have this sink available during cabinet construction because of the way it is installed.

MORE APRON-FRONT

They also have sink that are seamless with the countertop like solid surface. See countertop section of this book.

BASIN SINK FINISHES:

Water spots may show on the shinier finishes.

If you like the look of a commercial kitchen, choose stainless steel.

CAST IRON WHITE— Cast iron—won't dent, stain, scratch, or chip. Available in many colors; can be custom shaped.

STAINLESS STEEL—durable, easy to clean, and can be installed under-counter or self-rimming. Stainless steel is measured by metal content and thickness (gauge). Sinks that are 304 stainless steel (18% chromium, 8% nickel) are stain- and corrosion-resistant. The lower the gauge, the thicker the material. The best sinks are 18-19 gauge stainless steel.

GRANITE COMPOSITE—very popular now because it is scratch resistant and very durable. Available in different colors in matte finish.

COPPER—look for sinks that are pure copper with no seams, and be aware that copper is a soft metal that will scratch and dent easily.

Disposal noise and vibration can be reduced by purchasing a sink with sound-absorption technology.

GARBAGE DISPOSALS

Disposals with a 1/3 horsepower motor are sufficient. Newer models are also available in ½ –1 horsepower models. How much do you use a garbage disposal? If you have a large family you will probably want to get a disposal with a bigger motor.

Disposal noise and vibration can be reduced by purchasing a sink with sound-absorption technology.

If you want to place the garbage disposals on an island and wonder where to install the switch to start it, they have a push bottom that can be installed in the countertop.

Don't forget to look at the Universal Design section of the book for more ideas on Plumbing fixtures.

GARBAGE DISPOSAL NOTES:

_____
_____
_____
_____
_____
_____
_____
_____
_____
_____
_____
_____
_____
_____
_____

PICTURES OF SINKS YOU LIKE, OR MARK THE EXAMPLES ON THE PREVIOUS PAGES

LIGHTING FIXTURES

General Lighting   Ambient Lighting   Task Lighting   Accent Lighting

Lighting is so important. It can enhance or worsen your décor. Don't skimp on this part.

The main goal here is to make sure you have a good source of lights for all the activities you are doing in your kitchen.

Make sure the metal you choose for the light fixture goes with your plumbing and hardware fixtures.

I recommend installing a dimmer wherever possible so you can brighten or darken the room as you wish.

If the shade on your light fixture is dark, the light will not be as bright. Lighter-colored shades give off more light. Keep in mind that fabric shades are harder to dust and clean than the glass ones.

Be careful with the placement of your light fixtures so you don't create shadows on your work surfaces. If you do end up with a shadow, think about putting task lights in front of your work area.

I will not elaborate on the styles of lights too much. I will concentrate more on supplying information on the kinds of light fixtures.

Make sure you have the right proportion for the size of your pendant lights or sconces. We want to avoid looking to small or to big for the space.

There are four kinds of lights to think about in a kitchen—general, ambient, task, and accent. The purpose of each type depends upon the function desired.

Electrical: Make sure you have enough plugs where you need them. You may need more for a TV and computer. You may also think about going with a wireless connection. Don't forget the satellite or cable for TV.

Again, go visit lighting showrooms to see what's new.

GENERAL LIGHTING—general lighting is simply to be able to get around your kitchen easily. This is the main light fixture of the room. This category includes recessed cans placed in the ceiling. If you don't have any recessed cans, then your suspended or attached light fixtures from the ceiling will be your general lighting.

AMBIENT LIGHTING — is more for creating mood. It won't interfere with your activities if you don't have it, but will create a great mood. Examples include sconces on walls or lights inside and above cabinets. It is very close to the accent category. The difference is accent lighting emphasizes something.

TASK LIGHTING — helps you read recipes or cookbooks, and brightens your food preparation area for cutting vegetables, mixing ingredients, or washing dishes. If you have recessed cans on the ceiling as well as the pendant light above the table, the pendant light can become a task light so you can see food better as you eat.

Task lighting examples are below wall cabinets, pendant or recess above the sink or cook top, and pendant above the island and bar area.

Task lighting below wall cabinets: Make sure you add a piece of molding (trim) below the wall cabinets to hide the light fixture as much as possible. You want to see the light, not the fixtures, and it will be easier on your eyes.

ACCENT LIGHTING—this is used inside cabinets to highlight dishes or a collection. Don't forget to insert glass shelves if you want the light to shine all the way down to the first shelf. There are also side light fixtures which give a more uniform light.

Accent lights above wall and tall cabinets. This is used to highlight collectibles such as artwork, flower arrangements, or architectural features. It will add drama to your kitchen.

Don't forget to look at the Universal Design section of the book for more ideas on lighting fixtures.

PICTURES OF LIGHTING FIXTURES YOU LIKE, OR MARK THE EXAMPLES ON THE PREVIOUS PAGES:

HARDWARE FIXTURES

Hardware for cabinets · Cabinet knobs · Cabinet pulls · Fridge or tall cabinets · Hardware for interior doors · Interior door's hardware

HARDWARE FOR CABINETS

There are so many choices for cabinet hardware in a kitchen; hardware comes in different sizes and materials, so it can easily become an overwhelming decision. Go look at hardware stores to see the latest choices. You will have fun looking!

Here are some ideas on how to narrow your choices:

First, look at your budget.

Second, look at the color of metal you chose on the plumbing and lighting fixtures. They should match the finish.

Then look at style. Some hardware looks more rustic, contemporary, country, etc.

If you are brave, look at some fun hardware to incorporate with the basic ones you selected. For example, choose different hardware for your island.

Keep in mind to buy a few of the more expensive hardware and place them where it makes sense, like in an island, hutch, or glass doors.

You can easily mix and match hardware collections. Just be careful with this process so it doesn't look messy.

Try to grip the hardware and see how comfortable it feels in your hand. Go with larger pulls, if you're not getting knobs.

The cost adds up quick because so much hardware is needed in a kitchen.

Hardware is like jewelry; it adds drama to your décor.

Don't forget about pulls for appliances like the fridge.

When replacing new hardware on existing doors and drawers, be careful about the existing holes. You won't be able to fill and hide them if you go from a pull (2 holes) to a knob (1 hole) unless you have your existing cabinets painted.

CABINET KNOBS

CABINET PULLS

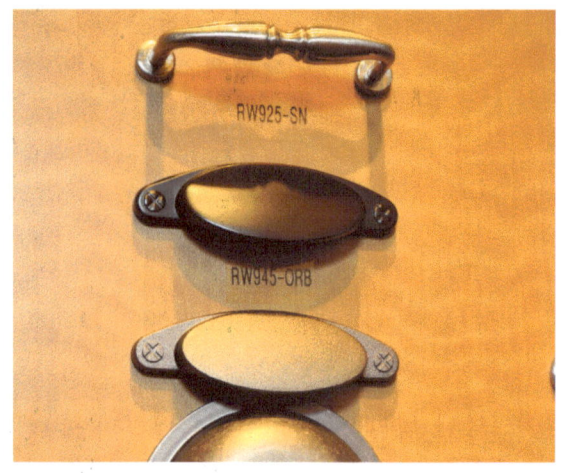

FRIDGE OR TALL CABINETS

HARDWARE FOR INTERIOR DOORS

Here are some ideas on how to narrow your choices:

First, look at your budget.

Second, look at the color of metal you chose on the plumbing and lighting and cabinet's hardware fixtures. They should match the finish.

Then look at style. Some hardware looks more rustic, contemporary, country, etc.

Try to grip the hardware and see how comfortable it feels in your hand. Go with larger pulls, if you not getting knobs.

INTERIOR DOOR'S HARDWARE

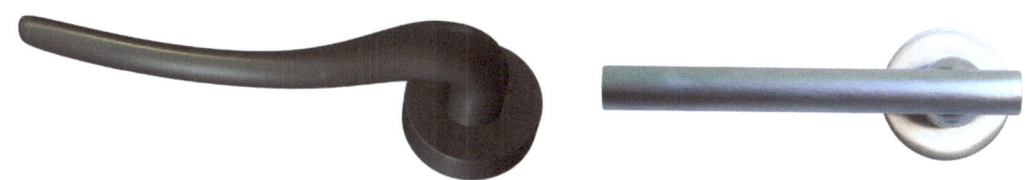

STEPS OF DISCOVERY OF MATERIAL

Don't forget to look at the Universal Design section at the beginning of the book for more ideas on hardware fixtures.

PICTURES OF HARDWARE YOU LIKE, OR MARK YOUR FAVORITES ABOVE:
_____
_____
_____
_____
_____
_____
_____
_____
_____
_____
_____
_____
_____

STEP 3: Architectural

Windows

Doors

Molding and trims

Ceiling and doorway treatments

WINDOW

It is so nice to have windows in the kitchen. Make sure you can open them.

You can always add a window in your kitchen. Just know that it needs to be consistent with the exterior look, not only the interior. Also make sure also you don't have any plumbing, electrical or mechanical inside the wall where you want to place your new

window. I will now start to elaborate on the style, the material and the color because there are so many options. Keep in mind to make sure they match the other windows, especially in the kitchen. Go look at a window store to see what is new.

DOOR

You may think of removing the door and replacing it with a doorway to get a more open feeling. Just keep in mind that the more open the kitchen is the more noise you will hear in the adjacent room. New doors will need to be painted or stained. You can also use a French door glass type.

If you have a walk-in pantry, you can get creative with the door or make it blend with the others doors in the home.

MOLDING

Here I am referring to the baseboard and the crown molding on the ceiling or chair rail on the wall. They will need to be painted or stained also.

CEILING AND DOORWAY TREATMENT

CEILING TREATMENT

If your ceiling is higher than 8' tall, you can create a custom ceiling treatment design.

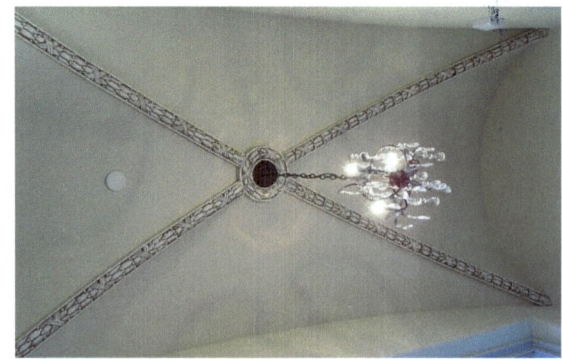

DOORWAY TREATMENT

STEP 4: Miscellaneous

Glass

Fabric

Luxury items

Technology

GLASS

Would you like to have glass cabinet doors in your kitchen? By using glass doors, you can show off your beautiful collections of dishes or glasses. Glass doors come in different textures. Go visit a glass company to determine how you will be able to see through it. If you don't want others to see what you have inside, choose a more obscure glass.

Because glass doors reflect light, they are great in dark kitchens. They also add focus and the cost is not very expensive.

They are available in clear or textured (obscured) glass. If you don't want to see what is inside the cabinet, choose a textured glass.

You can add light inside — it will also create a nice ambience and showcase your accessories if it is what you want to do.

Don't forget to get glass shelves inside the cabinet if you want the light to go from top to bottom.

PUT YOUR PICTURES OF GLASS YOU LIKE HERE:

FABRIC

You can use fabric in a kitchen for the window treatments, chair cushions, or tablecloths. Even though this book is more about kitchen remodeling, I thought I would include it in this book for you. This is where you can add pictures, or even actual swatches of fabric, to show the colors, textures, and designs you like.

PICTURES OR SAMPLES OF FABRIC YOU LIKE:

LUXURY ITEMS

Last, but not least, here's the space for anything extra you would like to throw in just because!

How can technology help with your kitchen design?

Technology is changing so quickly that, as soon as this book will be published, the information may become outdated. So just look at some ideas that you can research more on the internet. How can technology help us?

HOME AUTOMATION

It could vary from something as simple as remote or automatic control of a few lights or up to the entire house. You may also choose to install advanced controllers or use voice recognition. As a very basic definition, we can refer to it as home automation, because it gives you remote or automatic control of things around the home.

It could include everything from lighting control, surveillance, irrigation, whole home audio/video and more! Search Home Automation on the internet for more information.

INTERNET AND EMAIL

We all know the internet is an awesome and enormous library, and is free. Computers have made it so easy to communicate via email!

SMART PHONE

The new smart phones are incredible.

If you see something you like you can take a picture, save it on your phone, or forward it to your designer.

These phones make shopping so convenient. If you spouse cannot miss work, you can forward them the pictures of what you are seeing and ask if they like it. This will speed up the process since we don't have to wait for the approval of the other party involved.

We should not forget texting; it is a very efficient way to communicate short messages.

CAD (COMPUTER-AIDED DESIGN)

This is a great way to see what the kitchen will look like before it is started. You can make easy modifications to achieve the result your want. The designer will draw you a floor plan based on the dimensions of your existing room and all your needs and wishes for the project. From the floor plan they can view elevation or a perspective view to see the result better. See chapter 1 — Step 8 for example.

We need to embrace technology; it is here to stay so why not have fun with it?

BONUS: OUTSIDE KITCHEN

An outdoor kitchen could be simple like a barbecue grill only or elaborate like sink, appliances and flat TV. Look at your budget and see what you can purchase. Make sure the material is frost resistant. Your outdoor kitchen should use the same principles we use for the inside kitchen. Below are things to consider:

- Cabinets or wall stone or brick to support the countertop
- Countertop
- Maybe backsplash (Example: stone or brick walls)
- Flooring (frost resistant and not slippery)
- Appliances fixtures
- Plumbing fixtures
- Lighting fixtures
- Hardware fixtures
- Walls, ceiling and door
- Fireplace
- Electronic: flat TV and audio speaker

Don't forget to accessories and enjoy with family and friends.

MORE PICTURES OR SAMPLES OF LUXURY ITEMS YOU LIKE:

Congratulations!

You have completed everything and I hope you had as much fun with this as I have! If I can help further in any way just let me know.

If you are looking for ideas, please visit my website: www.sylviemeehandesigns.com. I've included resources on Universal Design, newsletters and blogs and information for all of us to share with each other. I will share with you what other people have written about their ideas and projects. I would love if people would send me their "before" and "after" pictures. If you want to ask me specific questions, I'll be very happy to answer them via my blog.

Welcome to my community of friends! I hope you have fun with this book as you put it together. When you're ready to start your project, share it with your designer. You'll be enjoying a new kitchen before you know it!

Sylvie welcomes your inquiries, comments, and reflections about Create the Kitchen of a Lifetime.

SEND INQUIRIES TO:

smeehan@sylviemeehandesigns.com
www.sylviemeehandesigns.com

References

THANKS TO:

Morrison Supply Company
311 East Vickery Blvd
Fort Worth Texas 76104
877-709-2227
www.morsco.com

The Bath & Kitchen Showplace
2910 N Stemmons Freeway
Dallas, TX 75247
972-630-6762
www.bkshowplace.com

Pro Source
5350 Airport Freeway
Fort Worth, TX 76117
817-831-8181
www.prosourcefloors.com

Photographers:
Jennifer Gilbert Photography
817-692-2396

Pictures Credits:
Kitchen layout diagrams:
www.kitchens.com

Kitchen faucets
www.Kohler.com

About the Author

Sylvie was born and raised in Montreal, Quebec, Canada. She came to Fort Worth, Texas, in 1996 with her family. Interior Design has been a passion of Sylvie's since she was a little girl. She loves helping her clients get the best out of their space by designing interiors reflective of their personal style. Design is an art that can sometimes be overwhelming and troublesome, but Sylvie Meehan can make it a wonderful experience every time. Sylvie received her Interior Design degree in Montreal, and brings with her years of experience in the design industry for new home construction as well as kitchen and bath renovations. She creates outstanding rapport with her clients by serving them promptly and efficiently, listening to their needs, and incorporating their own unique style into the design, all while staying within budget.

She also has a passion for helping others. She is a volunteer for Universal Health Services in Fort Worth, Texas. Sylvie goes to the homes of elderly people to help them by providing respite for the caregiver, running errands, listening, and simply being a presence for someone in need.

She belongs to the National Kitchen and Bathroom Association and the Greater Fort Worth Builders Association. Sylvie is a Certified Aging-In-Place Specialist (CAPS).

www.ingramcontent.com/pod-product-compliance
Lightning Source LLC
Chambersburg PA
CBHW060812010526
44117CB00002B/10